SIMPLE RECIPES THAT SAVE TIME AND MONEY WITHOUT SACRIFICING FLAVOUR OR STYLE

In her third cookbook, Christine Flynn takes decades of restaurant experience and distills it into simple strategies that anyone can use to enhance their culinary repertoire and confidence. *Easy Does It* is about doing more with less. Less effort, less time, less fuss, and less waste. It's about knowing which corners are worth cutting in the pursuit of mouth-watering food—without sacrificing the joy that comes from eating visually stunning and delectable dishes.

Christine's cooking puts practicality first. She encourages us to start with a sauce when dreaming up our next meal. Not only is a great sauce a springboard to creativity, it can make even the simplest of dishes stand out. Other strategies for streamlining everyday meals include pulling from the pantry when running to the store is beyond you, or celebrating the season's freshest produce by jazzing it up to create beautifully plattered dishes like Green Beans with Fried Lemon, Hot Honey, and Almonds. She brings a "breakfast for dinner" mindset to dishes like Skillet Eggs with Red Pepper Butter or Baked Eggs with Ham and Gruyère to keep weeknight dinners feeling achievable, and invigorates leftovers by transforming dishes like Braised Beef with Vinegar and Peppers into a crowd-pleasing pan of crunchy, cheesy, and slightly spicy Braised Beef Nachos.

If you're in a bit of a rut, Christine's knack for turning minimalist ingredients into maximalist results will bring creativity back to your cooking and transform your kitchen without adding a lot of effort. In *Easy Does It*, we see that mouthwatering deliciousness and efficiency really can coexist in the kitchen.

EASY DOES IT

EASY DOES IT
SMART TECHNIQUES
AND SIMPLE RECIPES
FOR STUNNING FOOD
CHRISTINE FLYNN

PENGUIN

an imprint of Penguin Canada, a division of Penguin Random House Canada Limited

Canada • USA • UK • Ireland • Australia • New Zealand • India • South Africa • China

First published 2026

Penguin Canada
A division of Penguin Random House Canada
320 Front Street West, Suite 1400
Toronto, Ontario, M5V 3B6, Canada
penguinrandomhouse.ca

The authorized representative in the EU for product safety and compliance is Penguin Random House Ireland, Morrison Chambers, 32 Nassau Street, Dublin D02 YH68, Ireland, https://eu-contact.penguin.ie

LIBRARY AND ARCHIVES CANADA CATALOGUING IN PUBLICATION

Title: Easy does it : smart techniques and simple recipes for stunning food / Christine Flynn.
Names: Flynn, Christine, 1983- author
Description: Includes index.
Identifiers: Canadiana (print) 20250158019 | Canadiana (ebook) 20250158027 | ISBN 9780735241619 (hardcover) | ISBN 9780735241626 (EPUB)
Subjects: LCSH: Quick and easy cooking. | LCGFT: Cookbooks.
Classification: LCC TX833.5 .F59 2026 | DDC 641.5/55—dc23

Cover and book design by Matthew Flute
Cover and interior photography by Suech and Beck
Food styling by Lindsay Guscott
Prop styling by Andrea McCrindle

Printed in China

10 9 8 7 6 5 4 3 2 1

For my family.

CONTENTS

THE RECIPES

INTRODUCTION

When I started cooking professionally, shortcuts were frowned upon. I'll never forget "egg day" at my culinary school in New York, when we had to prepare all manner of egg dishes, from omelettes to meringues to soufflés, with no equipment other than a bowl and a large whisk. By the time the bell rang, the entire class was rubbing their aching forearms.

In the working world, the recipes I encountered were often long and complicated. At the French Michelin-starred restaurant where I was an intern, every step required precision and had to be completed *just so*: you didn't simply grab a carrot and chop it—you peeled it and pared it and only then did you dice it into precise ¼-inch (5 mm) pieces. I once picked up a box grater instead of a knife to shred some chilled butter for the pastry dough I was making and my chef looked on in disgust before declaring my approach—which yields perfect-sized pieces of butter for pie, biscuit, and pastry doughs—to be cheating since I was not chopping the butter by hand. In the first decade of my career, I learned the technical way to do things as a restaurant chef. But more recently, when my role has been more often that of a home cook—working without gourmet ingredients, fancy equipment, sous chefs, or much time—I've discovered that there are faster, cheaper, and often smarter ways of creating delicious food.

This book is a reflection of how I cook *now*. I've taken decades of restaurant experience and distilled it into simple strategies that anyone can use to build not just your culinary repertoire but also your culinary confidence. *Easy Does It* is about doing more with less. Less effort, less time, less fuss, and less waste. It's about knowing which corners are worth cutting in the pursuit of mouth-watering food. This book will teach you to find the sweet spot between utilitarian cooking and giving up your free time to toil away on long ingredient lists and complicated instructions. My hope is that you will learn, as I have, that deliciousness and efficiency can coexist in the kitchen.

Each chapter makes use of the strategies I turn to every day to make delicious meals—quickly—for my family. **Start with a Sauce** (page 13) will teach you how to keep a few versatile sauces, such as Green Crunch Sauce (page 30) and Spicy Vinaigrette (page 26), on hand so that you can cobble together a meal in minutes, while **Spread and Slather** (page 35) will help you get something like Caramelized Onion Dip with Harissa and Herbs (page 47) on the table to get the party going with minimal ingredients or time. You'll learn how to leverage the fearless mindset behind **Breakfast for Dinner (or Lunch or Breakfast)** (page 59) to create compelling dishes like Skillet Eggs with Red Pepper Butter (page 63) or Feta Custard Toast (page 78). Find the freedom to work with what's in season with **Platter Your Produce** (page 87) and consider making a hearty plate of Charred Cabbage with Kielbasa Vinaigrette (page 117) or a simple yet impressive Any Vegetable Galette (page 90). With dishes like Pepperoni Pizza Polenta (page 147) and Fast French Onion Soup with Crispy Gruyère (page 128), **Pull from the Pantry** (page 119) has you covered for times when the seasonal produce is a bit sad or a grocery store run is temporarily beyond you. **Bake, Bubble, and Braise** (page 149) will convince you that turning on your oven or stove is worthwhile. One-pot wonders like Pepperoncini Braised

Pork Shoulder (page 166), not to mention the simple perfection of a Hot Honey Salmon (page 153), will make you swoon. Swing for the flavour fences with **Make It Taste Like Takeout** (page 173), where you will find recipes like Dill Pickle Pizza (page 189) and Sub Salad with Mortadella and Black Olives (page 177) among all sorts of delectable, restaurant-worthy meals, minus the price tag. Finally, **Use It Twice to Use It All** (page 205) will coach you not just to take your leftovers to the next level, but to reimagine them into something entirely new—dishes like Braised Beef Nachos (page 231) and Chicken and Dumplings (page 223) will have you sidestepping leftover fatigue with ease. And, for the dessert-dedicated among you, of course there is a compilation of my favourite sweet things that don't require too much in the way of time or technique in **Don't Stress over Dessert** (page 237).

Along the way, you'll find Tips and a clever little feature I like to call Swap It. These are good recipes as they are, don't get me wrong, but I don't want you to be too dogmatic about following them if you don't have the exact seasoning that is called for or are short a cup of sour cream. The Swap It feature of this book will teach you to think about what an ingredient represents, and not what it is, so that you can source a reasonable facsimile from what is close at hand as opposed to having to dash out to the grocery store or, even worse, bypassing a perfectly lovely recipe.

Throughout, you'll also find I've spotlighted some of my favourite ingredients in hopes of helping you get to know potentially new ingredients, like labneh (page 42), that will improve your cooking, or even just teaching you canny new ways of using items you probably already have, like white vinegar (page 165).

Easy Does It is a book for anyone who wants to cook faster, better, and smarter, and with more tenacity. In cooking your way through this book, you will gain the self-assurance and even the enthusiasm to throw your cupboard doors open wide and think "I can make something delicious!" without major effort or expense. The path to stunning, satisfying meals is easier than you think.

SHOP SMART WITH THESE 5 TIPS

We all want to eat well, and this book is all about preparing the most delicious food with the least amount of effort. In many ways, this starts with how you shop.

1. MAKE A LIST

Scribbling down a few bullet-point notes before you head to your local grocer will streamline your shop. Find a way to create a grocery list that works for you. You may choose to focus on gathering ingredients for specific dishes you would like to eat, or you may start with key items you're on the hunt for. I like to write down each ingredient I need for the dishes I want to eat that week, roughly categorized based on the grocery store layout—dairy items together, fruits and veggies in another section, and so on. However you choose to organize yourself, head out knowing what you need and where in the store you need to go so you can get what you need and then get out!

2. DON'T BE AFRAID TO IGNORE YOUR LIST

While it's great to go into the grocery store with a sense of direction, it's important to be able to pivot if something looks particularly good or entices you with an unbeatable price. If you wanted to eat a Steak Night Steak (page 203) but pork chops are on sale, don't be afraid to make a swap and do a Chop Night Chop. If you can't find radicchio for Basic Bitter Salad (page 98), grab a few heads of endive or pick a different green and go in another direction. Be flexible and stay confident.

3. SHOP LESS

I love me a grocery shop, but in recent years, with three kids and a busy work life, I've reined in my gusto for grocery trips and made do with what's in-house. The result? Less food waste, a fridge that is easier to navigate, and fewer unnecessary or excessive impulse buys. Shop less often and you'll find yourself saving money and time in a meaningful way. Which brings us to the next tip. . .

4. EMBRACE SHELF-STABLE AND FROZEN FOODS

Leaning on staples like canned tomatoes, jarred red peppers, tinned fish, and frozen peas has enabled me to cut way back on how often I head to the grocery store. Keep quality foods that won't go bad on hand and you'll always be able to knock together something that satisfies a craving.

5. PUT IT AWAY PROPERLY

This might seem obvious, but I can attest to it being easier said than done. Take a few moments when you get home from grocery shopping to unpack and organize your purchases and place anything you need to use up first in your immediate line of sight. If possible, use clear containers to store leftovers. Otherwise, a felt tip pen and some masking tape are all you need to clearly label things.

INVEST IN THESE 5 INGREDIENTS TO ELEVATE THE ORDINARY

Good food doesn't have to be complicated. Think of how satisfying garden-fresh tomatoes with a drizzle of extra-virgin olive oil, salt, and a little black pepper are. Or how fantastic a piece of charred bread slathered in good butter can be. If you spend a bit more on the ingredients below in the name of quality, you'll find you can always make something that tastes very good, very fast.

1. EXTRA-VIRGIN OLIVE OIL

Buy an extra-virgin olive oil that's been harvested within the last year. It will cost a bit more because it's likely been air-shipped instead of travelling by boat, but there will be a big payoff in flavour and health benefits.. Use it to turn greens into a salad, give a bit of gravitas to some poached fish before you serve it, or transform canned beans and bread into a compelling appetizer. In this book I call for extra-virgin olive oil as well as simply "olive oil," which can be a basic, more modestly priced item. Tip: where I used to use canola or grapeseed oil as a neutral-flavoured option to sear fish, whip into dressings, and oil my rising doughs, I now use a basic olive oil. This means I only need two kinds of oil on hand—unless of course a recipe requires butter, which brings us to the next ingredient!

2. BUTTER

Grass-fed butter is one of life's great pleasures and we all need as much pleasure as we can get. Feel free to save the premium stuff for spreading on bread or coating roasted vegetables and buy regular old supermarket butter for cooking and baking. However, you will notice a dramatic increase in the quality of your cooking if you invest in the best when it comes to butter. In our house we use a local 84% butterfat butter, and we always opt for unsalted.

3. CULTURED DAIRY PRODUCTS (CHEESE AND YOGURT)

I recommend you opt for really great full-fat dairy whenever possible. With ingredients like cheese and plain yogurt on hand, you'll always be able to add richness, tang, and even balance to any dish. Spend a little more on aged pecorino, soft burrata, and of course labneh (page 42), and you'll be ready to enhance whatever produce is on sale or elevate the long-lost bag of pasta that emerges from your cupboard just in time to save Thursday night's dinner.

4. FLOUR

While this is not a baking book per se, there is some baking involved, and I encourage you to find a good supplier for freshly-milled all-purpose flour that you can use to whip up all manner of cookies, cakes, and galettes of course, but also use here and there to thicken sauces, dredge cutlets, and even go all out and make Labneh and Scallion Stuffed Flatbreads with Spicy Oil (page 183). A higher quality all-purpose flour will have a fresh, slightly nutty taste, and provide more nutrient density and better flavour in your baking.

5. BREAD

Bread—and its slightly more tanned iteration, toast—can partner with just a single egg, or maybe a handful of mushrooms, or a steaming bowl of Chicken Broth (page 220) and become something incredibly satisfying. Good bread offers chew, crackly-crunchy crust, and, of course, the absorbency needed to mop up great flavours and carry them to your mouth. The best bread is made from the best flour, which means it costs more and has a shorter shelf life. You will be rewarded, however, with better flavour, more nutrient density, easier digestion, and an all-around more enjoyable bread-eating experience. If you can't quite make it through a whole loaf of bread before it starts to dry out on you, simply cut your next loaf into halves or thirds and store what you're not using in the freezer in a zip-top bag until you have a need for it. Thaw your frozen bread at room temperature and then run it under the faucet for a second to get it damp all over. Wrap it tightly in either a paper bag or aluminum foil and place it in the oven. Turn the heat up to about 325°F (160°C) and cook the bread for 10 to 15 minutes until the crust is crunchy and the centre of the bread is soft.

SKIP THE KNIFEWORK WITH THESE 5 TOOLS

If you want to cook good food quickly, it helps to eliminate unnecessary steps when preparing ingredients, and it is often faster if you take a different route to the same result. Your most important tools in cooking are of course your hands, which can be used for anything from tearing lettuce leaves into bite-sized pieces to neatly snapping asparagus stems to crumbling feta. But there are also a few more tools that will allow you to leave your knife in the drawer and make quick work of ingredients that need to be diced, sliced, shredded, or puréed in a hurry.

1. BOX GRATER

For more than just cheese! Grate your stale bread heels (page 140) for perfectly imperfect bread bits ready to be gently fried, get just the right-sized pieces of butter for Any Vegetable Galette (page 90), or shred a leftover baked potato for Cod Cakes with Dilly Mayo (page 209).

2. KITCHEN SHEARS

Having a dedicated pair of kitchen shears as opposed to rummaging around in your junk drawer for scissors means you always have them handy to snip herbs, divvy up a Dill Pickle Pizza (page 189), cut a roast chicken in half, or trim parchment paper. Don't feel that just because you *can* use a knife that you always have to. My husband has taken this advice to heart and now he uses a sturdy set of craft scissors to chop up bananas for our baby. The results, while not visually appealing, are exactly what is required for a successful baby banana experience.

3. MICROPLANE

A microplane is a tremendously useful tool for zesting and fine grating, which is why this is a staple in many professional kitchens. Use it for hard cheeses, Cured Egg Yolks (page 77), finely grating garlic into soups and stews, and my favourite, finely grating dark chocolate over vanilla ice cream!!

4. HIGH-SPEED BLENDER OR FOOD PROCESSOR

Probably the biggest investment on this list, but with equally great payoff. Use a high-speed blender to purée smooth soups, creamy dressings, silky pots de crème, and more. Texture is such an important part of creating wonderful dishes and a blender will allow you to elevate your cooking while also reducing the amount of time you put in.

5. MANDOLINE

This tool will drastically reduce the amount of time and effort you put into slicing vegetables. I use mine to cut down on prep time for all the onions required for Fast French Onion Soup with Crispy Gruyère (page 128) or to quickly and beautifully slice crunchy things like radishes and fennel to toss into salads. Mandolines are extremely sharp, so make sure to use the included guard and always close the blade before you place this tool in the sink to wash or in the drawer to store.

START WITH A SAUCE

I CHOSE TO PUT SAUCES AT THE BEGINNING of this cookbook rather than the end, because I often find myself reaching for the recipes in this chapter as a jumping-off point for a great meal. If you think of cooking as a puzzle, condiments are the corner pieces, and pulling a jar of, say, Red Pepper Butter (page 17) out of the fridge has the potential to lead you more clearly down the path to a complete dish. Perhaps you have some wilty-looking carrots you can bring back to life with a good roast and a bit of salty cheese. Voilà! Red Pepper Butter Roasted Carrots with Feta and Herbs (page 93). No carrots? No problem—grab the same Red Pepper Butter (page 17) from your fridge, locate a handful of pasta, and make Cheesy Red Pepper Pasta with Crunchy Bread Bits (page 143).

Maintaining a strong roster of smart condiments makes pulling together a meal if not effortless, at least intuitive. A great sauce, infused vinegar, or drizzle acts as a springboard to creativity as you pull ingredients out of the fridge. It also deepens flavours during cooking and can add a final flourish, lifting a dish out of mediocrity and making it into something with a bit more panache.

In the spirit of keeping things easy, I've also listed a few condiments that, unless you have the time or the inclination, I recommend simply buying. You don't have to do it all, and I will always encourage you to put your effort where it counts. That usually means you won't be putting it into something that's messy, time-consuming, or just pointless. After all, Hellmann's makes a great product.

RED PEPPER BUTTER

MAKES ABOUT 3 CUPS (750 ML)

I love keeping a jar of this simple, smart, and super-economical condiment around. It's like tomato paste, but with a bit more depth from both the red peppers and the allspice, and it can double as a spread thanks to the butter that is beaten in at the end. Use it to make Skillet Eggs with Red Pepper Butter (page 63) or Red Pepper Soup with Limey Yogurt and Basil Oil (page 131), or put together a simple but effective pasta like Herby Feta Orzo (page 135).

You can also use it to great effect when you're improvising in the kitchen. I like to schmear it on a charred piece of bread and top it with something creamy like burrata or Boursin cheese and a drizzle of hot honey. You might also want to slide a spoonful of Red Pepper Butter into the steaming pocket of a baked potato jacket before loading on plain yogurt and chives. It's also great to stir into most puréed soups and chunky stews for added richness, and you can toss it with just about any roasted vegetable for punched-up flavour and luscious colour.

¼ cup (60 mL) olive oil
1 can (28 ounces/796 mL) diced tomatoes
2 jars (16 ounces/475 mL each) roasted red peppers, drained
1 tablespoon (15 mL) white vinegar
½ teaspoon (2 mL) ground allspice
2 teaspoons (10 mL) salt
½ cup (125 mL) unsalted butter, room temperature and cut into cubes

In a large skillet over medium-high heat, bring the olive oil, tomatoes, peppers, vinegar, allspice, and salt to a boil. Reduce the heat to a gentle simmer. Cook, uncovered, for about 40 minutes, stirring occasionally, until everything is quite soft.

Increase the heat to high. Stirring frequently, boil off any remaining liquid until the mixture becomes thick and jammy. This should take 7 to 10 minutes.

Scrape the mixture into a high-speed blender or food processor and purée until smooth. Let the mixture cool to room temperature, or stick it in the fridge for 10 to 15 minutes: it should be cool enough that it doesn't melt the butter. Add the butter and purée until the butter is fully incorporated. Transfer the mixture to a jar with a lid or other airtight container and refrigerate until ready to use or up to 2 weeks.

MAKES ABOUT 1¼ CUPS (310 ML)

¾ cup (175 mL) tahini
Zest and juice of 1 lemon
1 teaspoon (5 mL) salt
½ cup (125 mL) cold water

WHIPPED TAHINI

Tahini is a flavourful paste made from ground sesame seeds—for a bit of a deeper dive on it, flip to page 246. Combining good-quality tahini with water, salt, and a spritz of lemon is a game-changer: the result is a silky, creamy, luscious sauce. Whipped tahini is great for people who are lactose intolerant because it's more digestible than dairy and, as a bonus, it's rich in calcium. In addition to being part of many recipes in this book, whipped tahini is also great as a schmear under sunny side up eggs, spooned over chickpeas, or swirled into your favourite store-bought hummus.

Place the tahini, lemon zest and juice, and salt in a high-speed blender. Pulse to combine. With the blender running on medium speed, slowly drizzle in the water until it is fully incorporated and the tahini is pale and thick.

Store in an airtight container in the fridge until ready to use or up to 1 week.

Tip: The creaminess of whipped tahini is not so far removed from a good mayonnaise, and you can often use it in similar ways. Sometimes I'll blitz in a handful of fresh herbs, like basil and dill, half a lime, and a clove of garlic for a green goddess tahini to drizzle over a hearty salad. Other times, I'll purée in leftover roasted vegetables like carrots or beets and top the mixture with a little crumbled feta or paneer for an easy dip.

EVERYDAY VINEGAR AND OTHER USEFUL VINEGARS

MAKES ABOUT 4 CUPS (1 L)

Lean on white vinegar to create infused condiments with a dynamic range of flavours that will add oomph to almost any dish. Think of it as a flavour shortcut—when you reach for a vinegar that's already loaded with, let's say, herby-lemony-savoury goodness and splash it all over, for example, a big pile of extra-virgin olive oil–drenched green beans, you are getting *all* those flavours, but only using three ingredients. By making and keeping a small selection of useful vinegars, you'll get more and better flavour in your food, with fewer steps.

Make an "everyday" vinegar like I do, but don't be shy about using what's in season and being creative. I've included a few of my favourite recipes below, like Rhubarb Vinegar and Hot Vinegar. Where you can go from there is limitless: try adding a favourite herb, or a combination of seeds and spices. Fruit vinegars are lovely and can add a ton of dimension to a simple green salad.

I usually keep my vinegars in big, sterilized glass jars in the fridge with their contents intact, but you can also strain your vinegars and transfer them to pretty bottles as you wish. Be sure to use a clean spoon when dipping in and out.

EVERYDAY VINEGAR

This vinegar is my go-to staple. It contains both the sharp acidity of vinegar and the bright acidity of lemon, with savoury notes added from the onions, herbs, and peppercorns. Spoon it over Spiced Eggplant with Olive Oil and Vinegar (page 40), add it to Green Beans with Fried Lemon, Hot Honey, and Almonds (page 97), or pour 1 tablespoon (15 mL) over ice and top it with cold seltzer for a weirdly refreshing fizzy drink.

2 small yellow onions, peeled and halved
1 teaspoon (5 mL) whole black peppercorns
Small bunch fresh thyme
Handful of fresh flat-leaf parsley
Rind of 2 lemons
3½ cups (875 mL) white vinegar
Pinch of sugar

Place the onions, peppercorns, thyme, parsley, and lemon rind in a 4-cup (1 L) jar with a tight-fitting lid.

In a medium saucepan, bring the vinegar and sugar to a boil. Carefully pour the mixture into the jar. Let cool to room temperature. Screw on the lid and store in the fridge until ready to use or up to 6 months.

SWAP IT

HOT VINEGAR

Hot Vinegar adds the best zhuzh to Pepperoncini Pork Tacos (page 228), is great splashed onto regular old fried eggs, and makes Crunchy Brussels Sprout and Raw Corn Salad (page 94) a little extra spicy.

Loosely pack a jar, with a tight-fitting lid, with 3 cups (750 mL) sliced hot peppers—you can use jalapeño, poblano, banana, Scotch bonnet, or a combination of the above. In a medium saucepan, bring 3 cups (750 mL) white vinegar and a pinch of sugar to a boil. Carefully pour the mixture into the jar. Let cool to room temperature. Screw on the lid and store in the fridge until ready to use or up to 6 months.

CHIVE BLOSSOM VINEGAR

Try this in vinaigrettes, mixed into labneh when you make Caramelized Onion Dip with Harissa and Herbs (page 47), or instead of white vinegar in Chicken Adobo with Black Pepper and Soy (page 168).

Fill a jar, with a tight-fitting lid, with chive blossoms (the cute little purple pompoms on top of your chive plant). Cover completely with room-temperature white vinegar and a pinch of sugar. Screw on the lid and shake vigorously to dissolve the sugar. Place in the fridge until ready to use or up to 6 months.

LOVAGE OR CELERY VINEGAR

Lovage is a bright green vegetable that tastes a bit like celery. If you're able to find some, it makes a refreshing vinegar with a unique and wonderful, almost vegetal taste. If you can't find lovage, celery also works. Try this instead of white vinegar in Chicken and Dumplings (page 223) or Baked Salmon with Spicy Lime Vinaigrette Celery Salad (page 154), or swap it out for half the lemon juice in Crunchy Celery Caesar with Tonnato and Hazelnuts (page 109).

Fill a jar, with a tight-fitting lid, with roughly chopped lovage or celery. Cover completely with vinegar that's been brought to a simmer, while it's still hot, and add a pinch of sugar. Let cool to room temperature. Screw on the lid and transfer to the fridge until ready to use or up to 6 months.

RHUBARB VINEGAR

This is such a great way to enjoy springtime rhubarb all year round. Use this vinegar in Green Beans with Fried Lemon, Hot Honey, and Almonds (page 97) or add a splash to the Herby Salad that goes with your Cheesy Dutch Baby (page 85).

Fill a jar, with a tight-fitting lid, with roughly chopped rhubarb. Cover completely with white vinegar, that's been brought to a simmer, while it's still hot, and add a pinch of sugar. Let cool to room temperature. Screw on the lid and transfer to the fridge until ready to use or up to 6 months.

HONEY HARISSA

MAKES ABOUT 2¼ CUPS (550 ML)

This condiment is so simple to make. It consists of toasted spices and some chilies puréed in oil, vinegar, and honey, and it packs a huge flavour punch. Pair it with eggs, fish, meat, vegetables, plain yogurt, rice, cheese, whatever! The possibilities are endless.

15 guajillo chilies
1 tablespoon (15 mL) cumin seeds, toasted
1 tablespoon (15 mL) coriander seeds, toasted
1 tablespoon (15 mL) Aleppo pepper
2 tablespoons (30 mL) sweet paprika
2 tablespoons (30 mL) pure liquid honey
1 tablespoon (15 mL) kosher salt
¼ cup (60 mL) white vinegar
2 cups (500 mL) olive oil

Soak the chilies in a small bowl of room-temperature water for 20 minutes so that they soften, then drain them. Remove the stems and do your best to remove seeds, but don't stress over it.

Place the chilies, cumin seeds, coriander seeds, Aleppo pepper, paprika, honey, kosher salt, and vinegar in a high-speed blender and purée. Add the olive oil and pulse to combine.

Store in an airtight container in the fridge for up to 1 month.

MAKES ABOUT 1 CUP (250 ML)

- ½ cup (125 mL) Honey Harissa (page 25)
- 1 teaspoon (5 mL) Aleppo pepper
- 2 teaspoons (10 mL) sugar or pure liquid honey
- 2 tablespoons (30 mL) white vinegar or Everyday Vinegar (page 21)
- ½ cup (125 mL) olive oil
- Juice of ½ lemon

SPICY VINAIGRETTE

This is a quick, vibrant, and tasty vinaigrette without too much heat. Drizzle it over wilted greens, roasted vegetables, or a piece of fish to add both flavour and colour.

In a large skillet over medium-high heat, warm the honey harissa, Aleppo pepper, sugar, and vinegar until the sugar dissolves and the mixture is just about to boil. Add the olive oil. Whisk to combine. Cook for 1 minute more, then remove from the heat. Stir in the lemon juice.

Transfer the mixture to an airtight container and store in the fridge until ready to use. This vinaigrette keeps indefinitely, just be sure to use a clean spoon when you dip into the container.

BASIL OIL

MAKES ABOUT 2 CUPS (500 ML)

7 big bunches fresh basil with stems (see Swap It)

2 cups (500 mL) avocado or olive oil

I make big batches of basil oil in the summer, when this fragrant herb is abundant, and then freeze it in ice cube trays to give myself a little taste of summer all year round. We drizzle Basil Oil on just about everything, from salads to soups to pizzas, and it adds both flavour and a beautiful bright green colour. Although it takes a bit of time to prepare, the recipe isn't complicated, and the ingredient list is simply basil and oil.

Prepare an ice bath by filling a medium bowl about one-third of the way with ice cubes. Add cold water until the bowl is two-thirds full.

Bring a large pot of salted water to a boil. Place the basil into the boiling water for about 5 to 10 seconds, until it turns bright green. Using a slotted spoon or a spider, scoop the basil out of the boiling water and plunge it into the ice bath until it has fully cooled.

Using your hands, squeeze the basil tightly to remove all excess water. It should be tightly packed and resemble a dark green tennis ball. Transfer the basil to a high-speed blender. Add the avocado oil. Purée for 2 to 3 minutes on high speed, until the basil is bright green and fully incorporated into the oil. Place a coffee filter over a fine mesh strainer. Strain the oil to remove the solids. If you feel there is some water remaining, freeze the basil oil. The water and oil will separate and you can discard the frozen water.

Transfer the oil to a jar with a tight-fitting lid and store in the fridge for up to 3 weeks. Alternatively, fill an ice cube tray with the oil. Once the oil is frozen, transfer the cubes to a zip-top bag and store in the freezer indefinitely, until ready to use. To thaw, simply place a cube in a small dish or jar in the fridge overnight.

Swap It: If you're short on basil, you can use other soft herbs and greens, such as chives, arugula, or Italian parsley, to make up the difference. You want something soft not just in texture but also in flavour: more powerful herbs like rosemary or mint will really take over, so stick to milder flavour profiles when reaching for a substitute.

MAKES ABOUT 1 CUP (250 ML)

- ¼ cup (60 mL) walnuts, toasted and chopped
- 2 cups (500 mL) fresh flat-leaf parsley with stems, finely chopped
- Zest and juice of 1 lemon
- Splash of Everyday Vinegar (page 25) or white vinegar
- ¼ cup (60 mL) extra-virgin olive oil
- Pinch of salt

GREEN CRUNCH SAUCE

My friend Matt Ravenscroft cooks some of the most incredible food out there and, like me, he focuses on lots of vegetables, big flavours, and simple techniques. This Green Crunch Sauce is one of his creations and it's become a favourite in our household too. It has great texture from the walnuts and parsley stems, but also acidity and herby brightness. Try it on Butter Bean Spread with Green Crunch Sauce (page 39), refresh leftover steak with it in Herby Sliced Steak with Feta, Baby Gem, and Radishes (page 235), or spoon some over roasted chicken, fish, or vegetables to add a little something extra.

Place all the ingredients in a small bowl. Stir to combine.

Store in an airtight container in the fridge until ready to use or up to about 1 week. The sauce will fade to a less vibrant green, but it will still taste just as good.

Swap It: No walnuts? Go ahead and use an equal amount of some other kind of seed or nut, like pumpkin seeds, pistachios, or even macadamia nuts. You're looking for anything crunchy and fatty to play the role of the walnut.

Swap out the parsley for herbs like cilantro, arugula, or mint for another spin on this simple and delicious condiment.

Change the acid component by using half an orange or a large lime instead of a lemon, or by skipping the fresh citrus altogether and doubling down on vinegar. There are endless variations! And! If you like this sauce, check out my riff on one of Matt's other iconic dishes, Garlicky Eggplant with Sesame Romesco and Herbs (page 113).

THE CONDIMENTS YOU SHOULD BUY

When it comes to making the most out of your time in the kitchen, cutting a corner or two is not just allowed but encouraged. Incorporating quality condiments made by brands that have their recipes down pat is a great way to let go of some of the heavy lifting so you can focus on the parts of cooking you enjoy most and fast-track your way to a great meal.

MAYONNAISE/AIOLI

I did a lot of things when I was younger that no longer fit my lifestyle. One of them was to make mayonnaise from scratch. So I will say, dear reader, if you are young or ambitious or a combination of both and you want to make your own mayo, go for it. It's actually pretty straightforward and you can find recipes for it in both of my previous books. Would I do it today? No, I would not. I would buy Hellmann's, Heinz, or, if I am lucky enough to be in a place where it is available, Duke's, because they are all terrific and no one is going to know the difference.

HOT HONEY

Hot honey is in heavy use in my household but I rarely make it at home because I find it's a sticky mess once you strain the spices out. Of course, I'm going to recommend my own brand of hot honey, Buzz, which is made in partnership with Zing Pantry Shortcuts. It's available across Canada and the United States and has both spice and a touch of acidity (from vinegar), which gives it great balance and consistency. I put Buzz on just about everything, from Feta Custard Toast (page 78) to Hot Honey Salmon (page 153) and Dill Pickle Pizza (page 189).

CHILI CRISP

I love chili crisp and there are so many great ones out there. I find it way more enjoyable trying all the different ones than carefully slicing garlic and shallots and simmering them in oil until they are *perfectly golden brown.* (I am also human and have flubbed this step more than a few times. Burning all of your carefully sliced garlic and shallots can really put you in a mood, so I recommend avoiding it.) My current chili crisp obsessions are Fly By Jing and Super Magic Taste. You'll find me using chili crisp to heat up Spicy Crunch Noodles (page 196); I also like to spoon it into a skillet while I fry eggs or drizzle it over Rice Cakes with Crispy Pork and Soy (page 199).

CRISPY ONIONS

You can of course make these, with or without dusting them in flour, in a pot on the stove, or in a large glass measuring cup in the microwave. Either way, you will spend a good deal of time slicing or mandolining the onions and an unreasonable amount of oil, which you then have to keep in a jar cluttering up your fridge until the next time you want to fry onions. And you will, without fail, at some point burn the onions and the whole exercise will be fruitless and frustrating. Do what I do and buy the crispy onions—with the confidence of someone who *knows they could make them*, but has better things to do.

IS NO
FRIEND OF

SPREAD AND SLATHER

SPREADS, SCHMEARS, AND DIPS have always been good-mood foods for me. At picnics and parties I make a beeline for anything slatherable in a pumpernickel bowl, and I have fond memories of my mother opening a packet of Lipton Onion Soup Mix and shaking the powdery contents into a bowl of sour cream to make what I considered for a very long time to be her own signature recipe for French onion dip. As the number-one mealmaker in my household, I also love dips because they are easy to make, and everyone seems to tuck into them without hesitation. If you have something dippy, you have the start of a great meal. It's no great effort to assemble a few things around a dip for an eating experience that taps into the kid in all of us and feels more like an all-night party and less like a busy Tuesday night.

Try Marinated Feta (page 51) sidled up to some grilled or roasted veggies and a pot of rice, or put out Surf and Turf Charcuterie (page 52) next to a Basic Bitter Salad (page 98) and the kind of crusty bread that crackles between your teeth when you bite down. You can also get to know one of my favourite ingredients, labneh (page 42), and try a few different approaches to make it into a show-stopping starter, including a Caramelized Onion Dip with Harissa and Herbs (page 47) that isn't much more complicated than my mother's take and has become a weekly staple in our household for all its wonderful textures and creamy more-ishness.

This chapter features effortlessly elegant dishes to slather and spoon on all sorts of things, made using easy-to-source ingredients and familiar flavours, with a couple of tweaks here and there to add interest but not exertion. Try them all, and don't be afraid to colour outside the lines with your own additions and updates.

BUTTER BEAN SPREAD WITH GREEN CRUNCH SAUCE

SERVES 4 TO 6

I love any kind of creamy bean situation because even though it feels a bit fancy, it's economical in terms of expense and time. This version, which leans on a whipped tahini base to give it a bit of airiness and olive oil to add richness, gets a bonus punch of flavour and texture from Green Crunch Sauce (page 30).

1 cup (250 mL) Whipped Tahini (page 18, see Tip)
1 large clove garlic
1 can (19 ounces/540 mL) butter beans, drained (see Swap It)
¼ cup (60 mL) extra-virgin olive oil

To serve
Green Crunch Sauce (page 30)
Crudités, flatbread, or crackers

Place the whipped tahini in a high-speed blender. Add the garlic and beans. Blend on medium speed until fully combined. With the blender running on high, pour in the olive oil and blend until smooth. Transfer the bean spread to an airtight container and store in the fridge until ready to serve or up to 5 days.

To serve: Transfer the butter bean spread to a serving bowl or platter. Liberally spoon green crunch sauce overtop. Serve alongside crudités, flatbread, or crackers.

Tip: If you don't have Whipped Tahini (page 18) on hand, simply place about ½ cup (125 mL) tahini, the juice and zest of ½ lemon, ¼ cup (60 mL) of ice water, and a big pinch of salt in the high-speed blender and blend on high until creamy and smooth before adding in the beans.

Swap It: The butter beans in this recipe can easily be exchanged for white kidney beans (also known as cannellini beans), navy beans, or even chickpeas. You can also use about 1½ cups (375 mL) of cooked white or red lentils. A different pulse or bean will change the taste slightly, but it will still be a super-smooth, great-tasting dip that is big on flavour and covered in wonderful crunchy herbs.

SERVES 4

SPICED EGGPLANT WITH OLIVE OIL AND VINEGAR

1 medium eggplant
2 tablespoons (30 mL) + 1 teaspoon (5 mL) salt
¼ cup (60 mL) olive oil
2 cloves garlic, finely grated
2 teaspoons (10 mL) sweet paprika
1 teaspoon (5 mL) ground cumin
1 teaspoon (5 mL) ground coriander

To serve
Extra-virgin olive oil, for drizzling
Everyday Vinegar (page 21) or white vinegar, for drizzling
Charred bread

This dish—a gorgeous, spice-rubbed, roasty-looking eggplant swimming in a puddle of good oil and vinegar—is dramatic in its simplicity. I love to present it on a platter that's sort of plain and let the eggplant take centre stage, with some charred bread on the side in a supporting role.

Preheat the oven to 425°F (220°C).

Holding the eggplant upright by the tip, with its bottom on a cutting board, slice off just enough of one side so that it will lie flat when you roast it. Holding the eggplant with your non-dominant hand, with the cut side in your palm, use a Y-peeler to remove the skin from the side of the eggplant that is facing you. Place the eggplant cut-side down on your cutting board and score the peeled side in a cross-hatch pattern using a sharp paring knife.

Fill a medium bowl with lukewarm water. Whisk in 2 tablespoons (30 mL) of the salt until dissolved. Place the scored eggplant in the salty water and let it brine for 20 minutes at room temperature. Remove the eggplant and discard the brine. Pat the eggplant dry with paper towels.

In a small bowl, stir together the olive oil, garlic, paprika, cumin, coriander, and remaining 1 teaspoon (5 mL) salt. Rub the mixture all over the eggplant, making sure to work it into the cut flesh.

Place the eggplant with the cross-hatched side up in a medium ovenproof dish. Roast for 1 hour, or until the eggplant has collapsed and is tender all the way through.

To serve: Transfer the eggplant to a serving platter. Typically, I serve it whole, in the skin, but you can also use a big spoon to scoop all the soft eggplant meat into a shallow bowl. Drizzle with extra-virgin olive oil and everyday vinegar. Serve immediately with charred bread.

Store leftover dip—which makes an excellent sandwich spread—in an airtight container in the fridge for up to 5 days.

Tip: Double this recipe and use your eggplant leftovers to make Charred Eggplant Dip with Hot Honey and Toasted Sesame (page 45).

SNACK

LABNEH: THE START OF SOMETHING WONDERFUL

If you've never tried labneh, you are in for a treat. It's a full-fat thick Turkish yogurt cheese and, while you can make it by straining plain Greek yogurt, I prefer to purchase it already made. Labneh has a wonderfully creamy consistency and just a touch of tang, and it can be used in lieu of yogurt, cream cheese, and sour cream in most recipes, making it a real multi-tasker and space-saver in the fridge. I use labneh in all sorts of recipes, like Creamed Greens and Crunchy Bread Bits (page 110), Baked Eggs with Ham and Gruyère (page 65), and of course Turkish Eggs (page 73). You can also use it in places where you might like something creamy—on toasted bagels, next to pierogi, or under a bit of homemade granola and fruit. Labneh is also the best base for a schmear that I know of—it is thick enough to hold all kinds of mix-ins but isn't so sour that it overtakes other flavours. Use labneh in the following three recipes to jump-start some great appetizers that might appear complex but are really just a bit of this and a bit of that swirled into yogurt with some crunchy stuff on top.

CHARRED EGGPLANT DIP WITH HOT HONEY AND TOASTED SESAME

SERVES 4 TO 6

This recipe is rich, creamy, and a bit luxurious because of the sesame and hot honey topping. If you've planned ahead, you'll already have a Spiced Eggplant with Olive Oil and Vinegar (page 40) on hand. If not, you can take the time to make one, or simply use about 1 cup (250 mL) of roasted eggplant from a jar (see Tip).

1 Spiced Eggplant with Olive Oil and Vinegar (page 40)
1 tablespoon (15 mL) tahini
Juice of ½ lemon, divided
1½ cups (375 mL) labneh

To serve
2 tablespoons (30 mL) sesame seeds, toasted
Hot honey, for drizzling
Extra-virgin olive oil, for drizzling
Warm pita, Turkish bread, lavash, or crudités

Combine the eggplant, tahini, half of the lemon juice, and labneh in a medium bowl. Stir to combine.

To serve: Transfer the mixture to a serving bowl or plate. Top with the sesame seeds and drizzle with hot honey, olive oil, and the remaining lemon juice. Serve with warm pita, Turkish bread, lavash, or crudités to slather, scoop, or dip.

Store leftover dip in an airtight container in the fridge for up to 1 week.

Tip: Most Middle Eastern and international grocery stores carry jars or tins of roasted and peeled eggplant. If you come across them, grab a few for your pantry. It's easy to use and can be added to dips (as above), puréed into soups like Red Pepper Soup with Limey Yogurt and Basil Oil (page 131), spread on sandwiches, dolloped into Braised Lamb Shanks with Butter Beans (page 162), or added to pasta sauces for a bit of smoky richness.

clubmed

CARAMELIZED ONION DIP WITH HARISSA AND HERBS

SERVES 4 TO 6

When you really let an onion be an onion, you realize what a remarkable little vegetable it is, with its variety of uses, personalities, and admirable qualities. Here, the onion is caramelized and combined with just a little hit of acid before being tucked into rich and creamy labneh. A dollop of spicy Honey Harissa (page 25) and a scattering of herbs, as well as more onions—both crispy and green—bring it all together. I must confess, this is the kind of recipe I typically double since it goes so fast.

- 1 tablespoon (15 mL) olive oil
- 4 medium yellow onions, thinly sliced
- Pinch of sugar
- Pinch of salt, more to taste
- Pinch of baking soda
- 2 tablespoons (30 mL) white vinegar
- 1½ cups (375 mL) labneh
- Hot sauce (optional)
- Fresh cracked black pepper

To serve

- 2 tablespoons (30 mL) Honey Harissa (page 25)
- 2 scallions, thinly sliced
- 2 tablespoons (30 mL) crispy onions
- Handful of fresh herbs and greens, such as mint, basil, flat-leaf parsley, dill, or arugula
- Warm flatbread or crackers

In a large skillet over high heat, warm the oil until it starts to shimmer. Add the yellow onions, sugar, pinch of salt, and baking soda (see Tip). Cook for 10 to 12 minutes, stirring frequently, until the onions are soft and brown. Turn off the heat. Stir in the vinegar. Transfer the caramelized onions to a medium metal bowl and place them in the refrigerator to cool for about 10 minutes.

Remove the caramelized onions from the fridge. Add the labneh, then the hot sauce to taste (if using). Season to taste with salt and pepper. Using a spatula, stir until well-mixed.

To serve: Transfer the dip to a fancy medium-sized bowl. Use a wet spoon to smooth out the top, then create a small well just off-centre. Spoon some of the harissa into the well and drizzle the rest all over the dip. Sprinkle with the scallions and crispy onions, and scatter the herbs on top. Serve immediately with warm flatbread or crackers.

Store leftover dip in an airtight container in the fridge for up to 1 week.

Tip: Adding a pinch of baking soda to the onions when you cook them over high heat will help them brown more quickly. However, if you add more than a pinch, the onions will start to dissolve into more of an onion jam instead of browning and keeping their shape, which is what we want for this recipe.

SERVES 4 TO 6

CREAMY CUCUMBER SCHMEAR WITH EVERYTHING BAGEL SPICE

1½ cups (375 mL) labneh
½ medium English cucumber, grated
¼ small yellow onion, grated
2 cloves garlic, finely grated
2 pepperoncini, thinly sliced
1 tablespoon (15 mL) pepperoncini brine or Everyday Vinegar (page 21)
Salt and pepper

To serve

2 tablespoons (30 mL) everything bagel spice (see Swap It)
Basil Oil (page 29), for drizzling
Fresh cracked black pepper
Handful of fresh dill, lightly chopped
Bagel chips or sliced English cucumber

This is basically tzatziki, but with a bit more pep from the pepperoncini. It's perfect as a dip and comes together in about as long as it takes to assemble the ingredients, but it's also wonderful as a schmear on sandwiches or pitas. You can even add a dollop to some cold roast fish, or pair it with a poached egg and some vinegary lettuces for a quick meal.

In a medium bowl, combine the labneh, grated cucumber, onion, garlic, pepperoncini, and brine. Season with salt and pepper to taste and stir.

To serve: Transfer the dip to a serving bowl or plate. Top with the everything bagel spice, a drizzle of basil oil, fresh cracked black pepper, and dill. Serve with bagel chips or sliced cucumber.

Store leftovers in an airtight container in the fridge for up to 1 week.

Swap It: Should you not have a shaker of everything bagel spice on hand, feel free to reach for some other seed or crispy thing to put on top: think sesame seeds, poppy seeds, crispy onions, sunflower seeds, dried chilies, even a crush of salt and vinegar potato chips. We're just looking for a little texture here—even better (though not imperative) if there is a punch of flavour too.

MARINATED FETA

SERVES 4 AS AN APPETIZER

8 ounces (225 g) feta, drained
2 tablespoons (30 mL) white vinegar
1 cup (250 mL) Honey Harissa (page 25)
Olive oil, if needed
Warm bread and crudités, to serve

This version of marinated feta incorporates Honey Harissa (page 25) to add notes of cumin and chili plus a touch of sweetness, with a little extra vinegar to keep the richness in check. I like to put this out alongside lots of bread, Garlicky Eggplant with Sesame Romesco and Herbs (page 113), or a Steak Night Steak (page 203).

Cut the feta in half lengthwise and place it in a container with a tight-fitting lid. Whisk together the vinegar and harissa and pour overtop. The feta should be fully submerged. If it's not, top up the harissa mixture with a little olive oil. Place the feta in the fridge and let marinate overnight or up to 3 days before serving.

Place both the feta and its marinade in a bowl or dish, and serve with warm bread and veggies on the side for dipping.

Store leftovers in the fridge in an airtight container for up to 1 week.

Tip: Crumble leftover marinated feta into a hot skillet and fry some eggs on top. Or toss the leftovers with hot cooked pasta and a handful of chopped summer tomatoes.

SERVES 2 TO 4

SURF AND TURF CHARCUTERIE

This is an easy, elegant, and very Italian-feeling snacking situation. It pairs a simple and typical Italian condiment called tonnato, which is basically tuna mayonnaise, with salty cured meat, peppery arugula, and a drizzle of bright, good-quality extra-virgin olive oil. Serve it as a light appetizer for friends alongside a glass of chilled Lambrusco, and use either warm focaccia or a baguette to slather and scoop up all that tonnato goodness.

This recipe makes more tonnato than you will need but, the next day, you can simply use it to make Crunchy Celery Caesar with Tonnato and Hazelnuts (page 109) or sandwiches stuffed with prosciutto, arugula, and a few roasted red peppers.

Tonnato (makes about 1½ cups/375 mL)

2 cans (2.8 ounces/80 g each) light tuna packed in oil
Juice of ½ lemon
½ cup (125 mL) mayonnaise
¼ cup (60 mL) olive oil
1 tablespoon (15 mL) water, more if needed
Fresh cracked black pepper

To serve

2.5 ounces (70 g) Coppa di Parma or other thinly sliced cured meat, such as prosciutto or soppressata
Handful of baby arugula
Handful of briny green olives, such as Castelvetrano, pitted
Extra-virgin olive oil, for drizzling
Warm focaccia or baguette

Place a large plate in the fridge to chill.

Make the Tonnato: Place the tuna, lemon juice, mayonnaise, olive oil, and water in a high-speed blender. Season with pepper to taste. Purée until smooth. The tonnato should be the consistency of mayonnaise. If it's too thick, add more water, 1 teaspoon (5 mL) at a time, until desired consistency is achieved.

To serve: Remove the chilled plate from the fridge. Arrange the Coppa di Parma in a circle on the plate. Spoon about ½ cup (125 mL) of the tonnato on top. Sprinkle the arugula on top of the tonnato and arrange the olives around the perimeter of the plate. Drizzle everything with good olive oil and serve immediately with warm focaccia.

Store the leftover tonnato in an airtight container in the fridge for up to 5 days.

BURRATA WITH WARM OLIVE VINAIGRETTE

SERVES 4 TO 6

Burrata is a soft, fresh Italian cheese that pairs really well with just about anything. It's bland in a wonderful, companionable sort of way, kind of like that one friend who has no strong opinions, shows up exactly when you need them to, and gets along with everyone without needing to be the centre of attention. In this recipe I've paired it with a chunky, warm olive vinaigrette, which is loosely based on one of my favourite condiments, muffuletta relish. This is a spread that can be found piled on top of cold cuts on the eponymous muffuletta sandwich and is typically comprised of vegetables, olives, spices, and oil. This dish is so easy to put together and, unless you don't like olives—in which case I suggest you turn the page—I guarantee you will love it as much as I do.

¼ cup (60 mL) + 1 tablespoon (15 mL) olive oil
1 small carrot, diced
1 stalk celery, diced
1 cup (250 mL) mixed pitted olives, chopped
3 pepperoncini, sliced, plus a splash of brine
1 teaspoon (5 mL) dried oregano
Pinch of sweet paprika
Pinch of sugar

To serve

8 ounces (225 g) burrata cheese, drained
Pinch of salt
Charred bread

In a large skillet over high heat, warm 1 tablespoon (15 mL) of the olive oil until it starts to shimmer. Add the carrot and celery. Reduce the heat to medium-high. Cook for 2 to 3 minutes, until the vegetables are softened, stirring often so they do not brown. Add the olives and pepperoncini. Cook for 1 minute more. Sprinkle in the oregano, paprika, and sugar. Stir to combine, then add the pepperoncini brine and the remaining ¼ cup (60 mL) olive oil. Cook for 1 minute more. Turn off the heat and let the flavours steep on the stovetop for another 5 minutes or so.

To serve: Place the burrata on your favourite fancy plate. Use a sharp knife to score the skin of the cheese, and to open it up a bit to expose the fresh cheese inside. Season with a pinch of salt. Spoon the warm vinaigrette over the cheese and serve immediately with charred bread.

Tip: If you like olives, this is the vinaigrette for you. Make a double batch (about 3 cups/750 mL) and store the extra in the fridge in a jar with a tight-fitting lid for up to 2 weeks. Use it to spread on sandwiches (especially mortadella), drizzle over cold, poached leeks, or dip bread into. You can even spoon it over cured meat or use it to garnish a piece of cooked fish.

SERVES 4 TO 6

BEER CHEESE WITH DARK RYE AND PICKLES

If you've never puréed cheese, I am here to figuratively hold your hand and show you the way, because that is exactly what this recipe is and it is so, *so* good. There's not much to it, just cheese, beer, a bit of seasoning, and some blender magic. After that, it's all about the accessories. I love the combination of sharp cheddar, dark rye, sweet onions, and briny pickles. When eaten all together, this tastes like something you would get at a pub that's been around for centuries and has well-worn leather banquettes and serves slightly flat beer in cold pewter mugs. It's somehow a very masculine, very compelling, and bold sort of schmear. It's also a very useful recipe to have in your back pocket because it's a great way to repurpose cheese ends or give new life to a half-eaten cheese board that's been sitting in your fridge for a week.

8 ounces (225 g) sharp cheddar cheese, cubed
1 pound (450 g) mild cheese, such as mozzarella, provolone, havarti, or brie, cubed
1 clove garlic
1 tablespoon (15 mL) Dijon mustard
Fresh cracked black pepper
Pinch of sweet paprika
Dash of Worcestershire sauce
1 cup (250 mL) lager or Pilsner beer

To serve
Dark rye bread and pretzels
Thinly sliced white onion (see Tip)
Pickles, such as kosher dill or cornichons

Place the cheeses, garlic, mustard, black pepper to taste, paprika, and Worcestershire sauce in a high-speed blender. Add about half of the beer. Pulse to combine. Add the remaining beer. Purée until smooth. Because cheese varies so much in flavour, be sure to give it a taste and adjust the seasonings as desired. Transfer the beer cheese to an airtight container and store in the fridge until ready to use or up to 5 days.

To serve: Remove the beer cheese from the fridge, transfer it to a bowl or platter, and let it sit for about 30 minutes before you plan to serve it so it softens a little. Serve with rye bread and pretzels, thinly sliced onions, and pickles.

Tip: If you're serving raw sliced onions, always submerge them in a bowl of ice water for at least 5 minutes before using. This will remove some of their sharp flavour and leaves them tasting a little sweeter—and will make them crunchier too.

BREAKFAST FOR DINNER

(OR LUNCH OR BREAKFAST)

HERE IS A CHAPTER THAT EMBODIES THE PHILOSOPHY that perfect is the enemy of good and encourages you to just cook something very tasty, very quickly. You can do so by approaching your cookery with the same mindset you tackle breakfast with. Have you noticed how rarely people get overwhelmed by making breakfast? It's because breakfast forces you to think quickly, limit your ingredients list, and not muck about with too many pans. Whether you are indeed making dinner, or it's a swift lunch or even just a delicious nosh before you fly out the door to work, this is a chapter to be dog-eared and devoured.

This egg-heavy chapter is also useful and unique in that it offers many dishes suitable for one or two people, which I get a lot of requests for and often make use of myself. Even though we are a busy family of five, there are often nights when the kids are over at a friend's, my husband works late, or I've already eaten at work, and a simple dinner that doesn't hinge on a microwave burrito is exactly the thing required. Or perhaps we're trying to work our way through some leftovers, and I just need something fast and tasty to round out a meal. If a recipe speaks to you, and you do want to make a larger quantity of it, simply double or triple it.

Make a Two-Minute Omelette (or two) on Whole Grain Toast (page 66), toss together a Bacon and Egg Salad with Frisée (page 74) in as much time as it takes to poach an egg, or give in to the temptation of a Cheesy Dutch Baby with Herby Salad (page 85). Channel your early-morning self, the one that's still waking up, grabs just one or two main ingredients, and has no time for too much chopping or struggling with a can opener. Be the you who understands that, when it comes to breakfast for dinner, it's not just about eggs; it's about efficiency.

SKILLET EGGS WITH RED PEPPER BUTTER

SERVES 1 TO 2

This recipe is a study in simplicity and perfect for a satisfying and fast meal any time of day. It can also easily be doubled or tripled depending on your needs.

1 tablespoon (15 mL) olive oil
¾ cup (175 mL) Red Pepper Butter (page 17)
2 tablespoons (30 mL) water, divided
2 eggs
2 tablespoons (30 mL) labneh or plain Greek yogurt
Zest and juice of ½ lime
Salt and fresh cracked black pepper
Spicy Vinaigrette (page 26)
Sourdough toast, to serve

In a medium skillet over medium-high heat, warm the olive oil until it starts to shimmer. Add the red pepper butter and 1 tablespoon (15 mL) of the water. Stir until the red pepper butter loosens into the consistency of a thick tomato sauce. Crack the eggs into the pan so that the whites aren't touching. Reduce the heat to medium-low. Let the eggs cook for 2 to 4 minutes, until the whites are set and the yolks are runny. Remove from the heat.

In a small bowl, whisk together the labneh, lime zest and juice, and remaining 1 tablespoon (15 mL) water. If the labneh is still quite thick, add an additional 1 tablespoon (15 mL) of water. The mixture should be the consistency of heavy cream.

To serve, season the eggs with salt and pepper to taste. Spoon the limey yogurt overtop, then Spicy Vinaigrette (page 26) to taste. Serve immediately with toast.

BAKED EGGS WITH HAM AND GRUYÈRE

SERVES 4

Leeks, ham, and Gruyère cheese are a classic combination. Here, with the addition of eggs and cream, they become a small but substantial dish. You can serve them with buttered toast soldiers and a big salad on a busy weeknight, or make them fancy and luxe with a dollop of caviar on top and some thin slices of crisp baguette on the side for an unforgettable start to a dinner party.

3 tablespoons (45 mL) unsalted butter, divided
½ cup (125 mL) diced ham (see Tip)
1 leek, white part only, thinly sliced
Pinch of salt
1 cup (250 mL) heavy (35%) cream
½ cup (125 mL) labneh
¼ cup (60 mL) grated Gruyère or Swiss cheese
4 eggs
Fresh cracked black pepper

To serve

2 tablespoons (30 mL) finely chopped fresh chives
Parmesan cheese, finely grated, to garnish
Black caviar (optional)
Buttered white toast

Preheat the oven to 375°F (190°C).

In a medium cast-iron skillet over medium-high heat, melt the butter. Use a pastry brush to brush about 1 tablespoon (15 mL) of the melted butter into four 4-ounce (125 mL) ovenproof ramekins, ceramic cups, or small bowls.

Place the diced ham in the skillet with the remaining melted butter. Continue to fry gently over medium-high heat until the ham has a bit of a tan, about 2 to 3 minutes. Use a slotted spoon to remove the ham and divide it evenly among the prepared ramekins.

Place the leeks in the skillet with the salt. Reduce the heat to medium. Cook for 3 to 5 minutes, stirring occasionally, so that they cook but do not brown. Add the cream. Reduce the heat to a simmer. Cook until the cream reduces by about half. Gently whisk the labneh into the cream and leek mixture. Spoon about half of the mixture into the ramekins, dividing it evenly. Sprinkle the Gruyère on top. Crack an egg into each ramekin. Spoon the remaining cream mixture on top. Finish with black pepper.

Place the ramekins in a shallow, ovenproof dish that will hold about 2 inches (5 cm) of water. Fill a pitcher or a large jar with warm (not hot) water. Pour the water into the dish holding the ramekins, so that water reaches about halfway up the sides of the ramekins. Place the dish in the oven. Bake for 12 to 15 minutes, until the egg yolks are just set.

To serve: Gently remove the ramekins from the water bath. Sprinkle the chives and a flurry of Parmesan on top. If you happen to have caviar, now is the time to pop the top and spoon a bit on each dish. Serve immediately with buttered toast.

Swap It: Try replacing the ham with a more or less equal amount of:
- mushrooms of all sorts, but especially shiitake, button, and chanterelle
- diced firm sausage, like chorizo or kielbasa
- leftover roast chicken
- smoked, cured, tinned, or roasted salmon or trout

SERVES 1

TWO-MINUTE OMELETTE ON WHOLE GRAIN TOAST

2 teaspoons (10 mL) unsalted butter
2 eggs
1 tablespoon (15 mL) heavy (35%) cream (optional)
Pinch of salt
Handful of grated cheese, such as cheddar or Swiss
1 piece of thick-cut whole grain toast
Fresh cracked black pepper

It's no secret that I think eggs are a perfect food: they are affordable, enjoyable, and quick to prepare using a myriad of methods. This is one of my favourite ways to make a simple but nourishing meal for one, but it's so quick to prepare that you can easily make three or four omelettes in no time at all. The cream gives the eggs a more delicate texture, but if you are short, you can skip it and your omelette will still be soft and luxurious, forming the perfect contrast to a crunchy piece of toast.

Melt the butter in a medium non-stick or well-seasoned cast-iron pan over high heat. In a small bowl whisk together the eggs, cream (if using), and salt. Once the butter starts to bubble and foam, quickly pour in the egg mixture. Reduce the heat to medium and cook for 45 seconds. Sprinkle in the cheese and let the omelette sit just until the cheese gets melty. Use a rubber spatula to slide the omelette onto the toast in a lovely haphazard bundle. Add a few cracks of black pepper. Serve immediately.

POACHED EGGS: A CHEAP THRILL, A LIFE SKILL

There are a few ways to poach an egg, including some that I would call more of a steam than a poach, some that require fancy cups or stirring techniques, and at least one method that asks you to use a microwave.

The way I poach an egg requires a pot, water, white vinegar, a teacup, and a slotted spoon. The vinegar helps the egg white set, and personally I like the way it tastes, but you can skip it if your eggs are both cold and fresh, since they will hold together better than an older egg that has been sitting at room temperature for any length of time.

It might take a bit of practice to feel confident poaching an egg, but if you follow this method, success is only an attempt or two away, and you'll be rewarded with an easy egg cooking technique that can elevate toast, complete a salad, or even make a soup stand out.

PERFECT POACHED EGGS

Line a plate with paper towels. Bring a medium pot of water to a boil, then reduce the heat to low to keep it just above a simmer. Add 1 tablespoon (15 mL) of white vinegar.

Crack an egg into a teacup or small bowl. From just above the rim of your pot, quickly pour the egg into the simmering water and set a timer for 3 minutes. If you are poaching more than one egg, now is the time to introduce them to the simmering water as well—just ensure you have enough water so that all the eggs can move about freely. In a medium pot you should be able to poach 6 to 8 eggs; any more than that and they will be too crowded, plus it will be hard to maintain the correct water temperature, which could throw off your cook times.

When the timer sounds, use a slotted spoon to transfer the egg or eggs to the prepared plate and blot off any excess water. Use the slotted spoon again to gently transfer the egg or eggs to where you'd like them to end up, like any one of the recipes that follow. Serve immediately.

SERVES 4

POACHED EGGS WITH ASPARAGUS, PROSCIUTTO COTTO, AND HOLLANDAISE

3 egg yolks
1 tablespoon (15 mL) white vinegar
1 cup (250 mL/225 g) cold unsalted butter, cubed
Juice of ½ lemon
Salt
1 pound (450 g) asparagus, ends trimmed

To serve
4 slices brioche sandwich bread, lightly toasted
4 slices prosciutto cotto
4 Perfect Poached Eggs (page 69)
Fresh cracked black pepper

I promised minimal fuss in this chapter, and I know you just read the word *hollandaise* and might have gasped aloud and said "I can't possibly make hollandaise," but I assure you that this is the least fussy version of hollandaise that exists and that yes, you absolutely can make it. Similarly, if you're considering bypassing this recipe because you have never heard of prosciutto cotto, it's just Italian ham—and available in most deli cases. If you can't find it, feel free to use regular ham instead. The dish will still be very good.

Bring a large pot of salted water to a rolling boil. While you're waiting for the water to come up to temperature, prepare an ice bath by filling a medium bowl about halfway with ice and adding enough tap water to cover the ice. Also, make the hollandaise by placing the egg yolks, vinegar, and about ¼ of the butter in a medium saucepan over medium heat. Whisk continuously as the saucepan heats up, so that the butter and the egg yolks fully combine. After 1 to 2 minutes, while continuing to whisk, add a few more cubes of butter. Keep whisking until the butter melts, and keep adding butter until you have added all of it and you have a creamy, pale yellow sauce. Whisk for 1 minute or so more to let the hollandaise thicken. Remove from the heat. Stir in the lemon juice. Season with salt to taste. Set aside.

Carefully drop the asparagus into the boiling water. Cook for 2 to 3 minutes, until it is bright green and crisp-tender. Use tongs to transfer the asparagus to the ice bath and allow it to fully chill.

Make perfect poached eggs (page 69) using a fresh pot of water. If you're in a rush, you can use the asparagus water: it just might make your eggs a teensy bit green, but you're going to cover them in sauce anyway, so there's no real harm in that.

To serve: Place the hollandaise over medium heat for a minute or two to warm it—be sure to whisk vigorously and don't walk away or it may curdle.

Divide the brioche among four plates. Ruffle up the prosciutto and place a slice on top of each piece of toast. Arrange the asparagus and poached eggs on top. Blanket each serving with a generous amount of hollandaise sauce. Finish with a few cracks of black pepper. Serve immediately.

TURKISH EGGS

SERVES 4 TO 6

This is a play on Turkish eggs, or çilbir, and it is breakfast for dinner in its very finest iteration. It's got eggs, yes, but it's also spicy, creamy, crunchy, oh-so-slatherable on a charred piece of toast, and takes just a few minutes to pull together and then enhance with fresh herbs and lovely bright celery leaves.

1 cup (250 mL) labneh
½ cup (125 mL) Honey Harissa (page 25)
½ English cucumber
Pinch of salt
6 Perfect Poached Eggs (page 69, see Swap It)

To serve
2 to 3 tablespoons (30 to 45 mL) Spicy Vinaigrette (page 26)
Handful of celery leaves
Handful of fresh herbs, such as mint, dill, and parsley
2 tablespoons (30 mL) crispy onions
4 slices charred sourdough toast, warm Turkish breads, or pita

Place a medium pot of water on the stove over high heat for your eggs.

Use a large spoon to schmear the labneh all over a large serving platter. Dollop the honey harissa on top and use the same spoon to spread the harissa around a bit.

Lay the cucumber on a sturdy cutting board and give it a few firm and satisfying thumps with a rolling pin. Tear the cucumber into bite-sized chunks with your hands and place the chunks in a small bowl. Season with a pinch of salt. Let rest for a few minutes while the salt draws out some of the moisture.

Prepare your perfect poached eggs following the instructions on page 69.

To serve: Gently place the poached eggs on top of the labneh and harissa. Strain any extra liquid off the cucumbers. Arrange them in some of the empty spots between the eggs. Drizzle with the spicy vinaigrette. Top with celery leaves, fresh herbs, and crispy onions. Serve immediately with toast.

Leftovers are better than you might expect and can be stored in an airtight container in the fridge for up to 3 days, though you may need to refresh the garnish with fresh herbs and crispy onions.

Swap It: If you aren't in the mood for eggs, this combo of labneh, honey harissa, spicy vinaigrette, little green leaves, and crispy onions is a great landing spot for all manner of things, from grilled fish to seared lamb, beef, or chicken and roasted veggies—especially eggplant.

SERVES 4

BACON AND EGG SALAD WITH FRISÉE

1 tablespoon (15 mL) olive oil
½ pound (225 g) slab bacon, cubed
2 tablespoons (30 mL) Dijon mustard
2 tablespoons (30 mL) Chive Vinegar (page 22) or white vinegar
1 tablespoon (15 mL) pure liquid honey
4 Perfect Poached Eggs (page 69)

To serve

1 small head of frisée lettuce, torn into bite-sized pieces
3 radishes, thinly sliced
Fresh cracked black pepper
Handful of chives, minced
1 Cured Egg Yolk (recipe follows on page 77)

This recipe takes its cues from a classic French salad called Salade Lyonnaise, which is typically a combo of frisée or other greens, like escarole and chicory, a warm, bacon-based vinaigrette, and a poached egg. It's a very good salad, and I never like to mess with a good thing *too much*, but I do like to add a scattering of thinly sliced radishes for some peppery crunch, as well as a little Cured Egg Yolk (page 77) for extra drama and a bit of *je ne sais quoi*.

Place a medium pot of water on the stove over high heat for your eggs.

In a medium skillet over high heat, warm the olive oil until it just starts to shimmer. Add the bacon. Reduce the heat to medium. Cook the bacon, stirring so that it does not burn, until it is just crisp, about 4 to 5 minutes. Turn off the heat. Whisk in the mustard, vinegar, and honey.

Prepare your perfect poached eggs following the instructions on page 69.

To serve: Place the frisée lettuce, eggs, and radishes on a medium plate. Using a large spoon, drizzle the bacon dressing over the salad, making sure the bacon is evenly distributed. Add a few cracks of black pepper and sprinkle chives overtop. Finely grate the cured egg yolk all over the salad. Serve immediately.

CURED EGG YOLKS

MAKES 4 OR 5 CURED EGG YOLKS

4 or 5 eggs
1 cup (250 mL) kosher salt
1 cup (250 mL) sugar

Cured egg yolks never fail to impress and they are a lot more straightforward to make than you might think. The egg whites that are left over can be used for another recipe, like Pistachio Cookies (page 255).

Separate the eggs, setting aside the whites for another use and being careful to keep the yolks intact.

Whisk together the kosher salt and the sugar and place about half of it in a shallow dish. Use the back of a spoon to make a dimple in the salt-sugar mix for each yolk to sit in, and gently transfer the yolks into each dimple. Cover with the remaining salt-sugar mix and let cure at room temperature for 6 days.

After 6 days, remove the yolks from the salt-sugar mix, rinse briefly, and place on a wire rack to air-dry at room temperature for a day. Transfer to an airtight container and store at room temperature for up to 3 months. Grate finely over pastas, salads, soups, toast, and more—really anywhere you would like a bit of interesting, funky flavour.

MAKES 2 TOASTS

FETA CUSTARD TOAST

- 2 slices thick-cut sourdough bread
- 1 tablespoon (15 mL) olive oil
- 1 egg
- 1 tablespoon (15 mL) heavy (35%) cream
- 4 ounces (115 g) feta, drained and crumbled
- ½ cup (125 mL) grated mozzarella cheese
- Hot honey, for drizzling

Custard toast is a symphony of textures, with an eggy, custardy top over crunchy bread. Although it might sound intimidating, this is an easy, delicious dish to make with just a handful of ingredients. This version uses a combination of cheeses, so you get all the salty brininess of feta plus a little stretchy pull from the melty mozzarella. The egg tenderly holds the cheeses together and also creates a wonderful mouthfeel that is very more-ish. Drizzle it all over with hot honey and serve it next to a pile of lemony baby arugula or a Basic Bitter Salad (page 98) for a quick meal that is both satisfying and decadent.

Preheat the oven to 400°F (200°C). Line a baking sheet with parchment paper.

Lay the bread out on a sturdy cutting board or clean surface. Use the back of a spoon to press down in the middle of each slice of bread to form a well, making sure to leave a ½-inch (1 cm) rim around the crust of the bread. Place the bread on the prepared baking sheet and brush the top of each slice with the olive oil. Bake for 5 minutes, until lightly golden.

In a small bowl, use a fork to whisk together the egg and cream. Stir in the feta and mozzarella. The mixture will be quite chunky. Divide the egg mixture between the two toasts. Return the toast to the oven for 10 to 12 minutes, until the egg mixture is slightly puffed and golden.

Drizzle the toasts with hot honey. Serve immediately.

SESAME EGG ON A BUN

MAKES 1 SANDWICH

2 tablespoons (30 mL) butter
1 tablespoon (15 mL) olive oil
2 tablespoons (30 mL) sesame seeds, divided
1 egg
Salt
1 brioche bun, cut in half
¼ avocado, pitted, peeled, and sliced
1 slice prosciutto cotto or ham
1 slice processed cheese
1 tablespoon (15 mL) hot honey
Handful of shredded iceberg lettuce

One evening when I was feeling tired and uninspired to cook, my husband, Oscar, surprised and delighted me with something he called "sesame egg"—a recipe he concocted during peak quarantine as a topper for instant ramen noodles. It's simply sesame seeds fried in a bit of butter with an egg cracked into the seeds and then topped with more seeds. The result is a stunning textural combo of runny yolk and crispy seeds, with incredible flavour that goes beyond a simple fried egg. I can't really explain it, but sesame egg is more than the sum of its parts. With a bit of further exploration and collaboration, we found that the best way to eat a sesame egg is in the form of a breakfast sandwich—but please do not limit yourself to eating these only in the morning.

Line a plate with paper towels. In a medium cast-iron skillet over high heat, warm the butter and olive oil in the centre of the pan until they just start to bubble. Add about half of the sesame seeds, reduce the heat to medium, and toast the seeds until light golden brown, about 1 minute.

Use the back of a spoon to make a small, yolk-sized indentation in the seeds. Crack the egg into a teacup or small ramekin, then quickly pour the egg into the sizzling seeds. Cook until the bottom of the egg white has set. Sprinkle the remaining seeds on top of the egg and use a spatula to flip it over. Continue cooking for 1 to 2 minutes, until the entire egg white has set and the sesame seeds are golden brown. Gently lift the egg out of the pan with the spatula and place it on the prepared plate. Sprinkle with salt to taste.

Use a paper towel to wipe out the still-hot skillet, then return it to the stove over low heat. Place the bun in the skillet, cut-side down. Toast for 1 to 2 minutes, until golden. Transfer the toasted bun to a clean plate. On the bottom half of the bun, layer the avocado, prosciutto cotto, and cheese. Place the sesame egg on the cheese. Drizzle everything with hot honey and top it with iceberg lettuce. Complete the sandwich by placing the bun lid on top. Serve immediately with lots of napkins.

SERVES 6 TO 8

LEMONY EGG DROP SOUP WITH TINY PASTA AND PECORINO

12 cups (3 L) Chicken Broth (page 220) or store-bought chicken stock
½ pound (225 g) little pasta, like stelline
4 eggs, beaten
¼ cup (60 mL) finely grated pecorino cheese

To serve
Extra-virgin olive oil, for drizzling
Fresh cracked black pepper
Juice of 1 lemon

This soup takes only as long to put together as the pasta takes to cook and it's always well-received by my whole family. A hybrid of two Italian soups—pastina and stracciatella—it's the best of both worlds, since it has all the heartwarming good vibes of a chicken noodle soup and the richness of an egg drop. I like to add finely grated pecorino to the eggs, which adds even more flavour and depth to this soup, and a squeeze of lemon to bring some brightness.

In a medium saucepan, bring the chicken broth to a boil. Add the pasta and cook according to the package instructions.

In a small bowl, whisk together the eggs and the cheese.

Once the pasta is cooked, turn off the heat. Use a large wooden spoon to swirl the soup and slowly pour in the egg and cheese mixture. Allow the eggs 1 to 2 minutes to set.

To serve: Ladle the soup into bowls. Finish each serving with a drizzle of olive oil, cracked black pepper to taste, and a squeeze of lemon juice.

Store leftovers in an airtight container in the fridge for up to 1 week. Reheat the soup in a small saucepan over medium-high heat. Bring it up to a simmer, but do not let the soup boil or the eggs will become tough and the noodles will become too soft.

CHEESY DUTCH BABY WITH HERBY GREEN SALAD

SERVES 4 TO 6

This combination of recipes is a very good one. It's essentially a big, cheesy, poufy pancake, partnered with a bright, herby, lemony salad—and both recipes require minimal prep. I like to put my Dutch baby in the oven, set the table, and then assemble the salad, leaving it undressed until I remove the Dutch baby from the oven so that the greens stay as perky as possible.

Dutch Baby

⅔ cup (150 mL) whole (3.5%) milk
2 tablespoons (30 mL) unsalted butter, melted
4 large eggs, room temperature
1 tablespoon (15 mL) Dijon mustard
⅔ cup (150 mL) all-purpose flour
½ cup (125 mL) grated Gruyère cheese
1 tablespoon (15 mL) olive oil

Herby Green Salad

3 cups (750 mL) baby arugula or mixed greens
Handful of fresh herbs (chives, dill, flat-leaf parsley, or basil)
Salt and fresh cracked black pepper to taste
Juice of ½ lemon
Extra-virgin olive oil, for drizzling

Make the Dutch Baby: Preheat the oven to 450°F (230°C). Place a large cast-iron skillet in the oven to get very hot.

Place the milk, butter, eggs, and mustard in a high-speed blender. Pulse to combine. Add the flour and purée until smooth. Add the cheese and pulse once to combine.

Using oven mitts, carefully remove the hot skillet from the oven. Add the olive oil. Swirl the pan so that the oil coats the bottom. Quickly pour in the batter. Return the skillet to the oven and bake for 15 minutes. Reduce the temperature to 375°F (190°C) and continue baking for another 5 minutes.

Make the Herby Green Salad: Place the arugula in a large bowl. Tear or use kitchen scissors to snip bite-sized pieces of the fresh herbs into the greens. Season to taste with salt and pepper. When you are ready to serve, dress the salad with the lemon and a glug or two of olive oil. Serve immediately alongside the hot Dutch baby.

PLATTER YOUR PRODUCE

I AM CONVINCED THAT EVERYTHING LOOKS BETTER ON a platter. I like the haphazard abundance and drama of a big pile of good food that hasn't been fussed over, even more so when it's set in a pool of something acidic, a bit creamy, or both. A crunchy touch, like some nuts, or bread heels transformed as if by alchemy—but really by a box grater, olive oil, and heat—into crisp crumbs, is also lovely but not always necessary.

This is a section for vegetable cookery that requires only limited knifework, simple techniques, and some prominent plates. You can expect short ingredient lists in recipes like Endive, Grapefruit, and Fennel Salad (page 106), punchy flavours leveraging smart condiments with dishes such as Spicy Roasted Cauliflower over Whipped Tahini (page 114), and familiar tastes reimagined in unexpected and enjoyable ways, as in Crunchy Celery Caesar with Tonnato and Hazelnuts (page 109).

The platter treatment is especially good for vegetables because it allows you to celebrate their inherent flavour and goodness. We're not trying to hide anything in this chapter: each dish has a focal point and that focal point, simply by virtue of the streamlined nature of these recipes, is always the vegetable in question. These are not recipes where carrots taste like beef fat, or we've somehow turned beets into a hamburger. The vegetables do the hard work and they shine while doing it. These recipes will encourage you to eat your vegetables, and to taste and enjoy them too.

MAKES 1 LARGE GALETTE

ANY VEGETABLE GALETTE

Pastry

2 cups (500 mL) all-purpose flour, more for dusting
Pinch of sugar
Pinch of salt
1 cup (250 mL/225 g) unsalted butter, chilled
1 egg, beaten
1 tablespoon (15 mL) white vinegar or pickle juice
1 tablespoon (15 mL) Dijon mustard
1 tablespoon (15 mL) ice water

White Sauce

2 tablespoons (30 mL) unsalted butter
2 tablespoons (30 mL) all-purpose flour
1 cup (250 mL) whole (3.25%) milk, warmed just to a simmer
Pinch of salt

Topping

1½ cups (375 mL) thinly sliced zucchini, or halved cherry tomatoes, or thinly sliced butternut or delicata squash, or thinly sliced something else
2 tablespoons (30 mL) extra-virgin olive oil, more for drizzling
1 teaspoon (5 mL) kosher salt
Fresh cracked black pepper (optional)
1 egg, beaten

This is a super flaky, no fuss pastry topped with a quick white sauce and then whatever thinly sliced vegetable happens to be calling your name at that moment. Zucchini, as pictured, is one of my favourites, but this dish is equally good with tender stalks of spring asparagus, a smattering of halved grape tomatoes in August, or even a layer of finely sliced butternut squash.

Make the Pastry: In a large bowl, whisk together the flour, sugar, and salt. Use a box grater to grate in the butter. Use floured hands to toss everything together. In another bowl, briefly whisk together the egg, vinegar, Dijon mustard, and ice water. Pour the mixture into the flour and knead briefly to combine. Once the dough comes together, use a rolling pin to roll it out until it is about 1 inch (2.5 cm) thick. Fold it over on itself, then repeat the process of rolling and folding again, sprinkling a little flour here and there if your surface or rolling pin gets sticky. Form the dough into a thick disk about the size of a side plate, wrap tightly in plastic or parchment, and chill for at least 1 hour.

Make the White Sauce: In a small saucepan, melt the butter over medium heat. Whisk in the flour. Continue whisking for 2 to 3 minutes, until the mixture looks dry. Whisking continuously, slowly pour in the milk. Continue whisking for 5 minutes, until the sauce has thickened. Season with a pinch of salt.

Assemble the Galette: Preheat the oven to 400°F (200°C). Line a baking sheet with parchment paper.

Roll out the dough into a rough circle until it is about 3/16 inch (4 mm) thick. Transfer it to the prepared baking sheet. Spoon the white sauce into the centre of the dough and use the back of the spoon to spread it evenly, leaving about a 2-inch (5 cm) rim.

In a medium bowl, toss your vegetable of choice with the olive oil, salt, and pepper (if using). Arrange the vegetable mixture on top of the sauce. Fold up the edges of the galette dough, but don't worry about making it look too perfect. Brush the edges of the galette with the beaten egg and place it in the oven for 25 to 30 minutes, until the crust is golden brown. Let cool for about 5 minutes. Serve. Store leftovers in an airtight container in the fridge for up to 5 days.

Swap It: Swap out the vegetables, yes, but don't be afraid to whisk 1 tablespoon (15 mL) of Dijon mustard, a pinch of ground red chilies, or even a ½ teaspoon (2 mL) of nutmeg into the white sauce. You can also add ½ cup (125 mL) of grated cheese to the sauce. I love adding melty mozzarella, a handful of sharp Red Fox, or even some crumbly Stilton to ramp up the flavour.

RED PEPPER BUTTER ROASTED CARROTS WITH FETA AND HERBS

SERVES 4

Carrots, along with celery and onions, are constant companions in my culinary adventures at home. At just about any moment, you'll find all three in my crisper because they are incredibly versatile in addition to being economical and long-lasting. When I cook, carrots work their way into stocks and soups, get turned into quick pickles for salads and sandwiches, and even find themselves shredded and baked into muffins and cakes. And when I am racking my brain for a quick side to go with a Roast Chicken with Pomegranate Molasses and Pistachios (page 158), a Steak Night Steak (page 203), or even a Hot Honey Salmon (page 153), I give them this treatment: I roast them, toss them in Red Pepper Butter (page 17), and then cover them in feta and herby Green Crunch Sauce.

1 large bunch carrots, tops attached
2 tablespoons (30 mL) olive oil
Salt
½ cup (125 mL) Red Pepper Butter (page 17)
½ cup (125 mL) crumbled Marinated Feta (page 51) or regular feta
½ cup (125 mL) Green Crunch Sauce (page 30)

Preheat the oven to 500°F (260°C). Line a rimmed baking sheet with parchment paper or foil.

Remove the tops from the carrots and set aside the nicest tops. Cut the carrots in half lengthwise and place on the prepared baking sheet. Toss briefly with the olive oil and season with salt to taste. Roast for 12 to 15 minutes, until golden brown. Transfer the roasted carrots to a large bowl. Toss with the red pepper butter and about half of the feta. Return everything to the baking sheet. Continue cooking for 5 minutes.

Wash and gently pat dry a large handful of reserved carrot tops. Roughly chop, so that you have about ½ cup (125 mL) of the tops. Add the green crunch sauce to a small bowl, then stir in the chopped carrot tops.

Place the roasted carrots on a large platter and top with the remaining feta. Drizzle with the green crunch sauce. Serve immediately.

Leftovers can be stored in an airtight container in the fridge for up to 5 days.

Swap It: This recipe invites, and indeed occasionally begs for, swaps depending on the season. In the winter: roast a few sweet potatoes, a butternut squash, or a small cabbage cut into wedges in lieu of carrots.

In the summer: try zucchini cut into thick planks or any vegetable, really, that might benefit from a quick ride in the oven and a bit of a flourish.

SERVES 4 TO 6

CRUNCHY BRUSSELS SPROUT AND RAW CORN SALAD

Dressing

- 2 pepperoncini, plus 1 tablespoon (15 mL) brine or Hot Vinegar (page 22)
- Zest and juice of 1 lime
- ½ bunch fresh cilantro
- 1 tablespoon (15 mL) hot honey or pure liquid honey
- ½ cup (125 mL) mayonnaise

Salad

- 1 red onion, thinly sliced
- ½ cup (125 mL) white vinegar
- ¼ cup (60 mL) sugar
- 1 pound (450 g) Brussels sprouts, trimmed and thinly sliced
- 2 ears fresh corn, kernels removed and cobs discarded
- 1 cup (250 mL) crumbled queso fresco, divided
- ½ bunch fresh cilantro, chopped and divided
- 1 avocado, pitted, peeled, and sliced
- 1 jalapeño pepper, thinly sliced

This salad, featuring loads of crunchy Brussels sprouts and fresh corn topped with crumbled cheese, rich avocado, spicy jalapeño slices, and acidic pickles, all in a quick creamy dressing, is the perfect summer side. It comes together so quickly—especially with the help of a mandoline for slicing (page 11)—and holds up great for al fresco dining. Pair it with Steak Night Steak (page 203) for my ideal summer meal, or serve it alongside Pepperoncini Pork Tacos (page 228) for a quick midweek dinner.

Make the Dressing: Place the pepperoncini and brine, lime zest and juice, cilantro, and hot honey in a high-speed blender. Pulse to combine. Add the mayonnaise. Purée until smooth.

Make the Salad: Place the red onion in a small heatproof bowl or jar. In a small saucepan over high heat, bring the vinegar and sugar to a boil. Pour the vinegar mixture over the onions. Let stand for 10 minutes, tossing occasionally to make sure all the onions have been coated with the pickling liquid.

Place the Brussels sprouts, corn, about half of the cheese, and about half the cilantro in a large bowl. Pour over the dressing. Toss well to combine. Transfer the salad to a large platter or serve it in the bowl you used to toss it. Top with the avocado and pickled onions. Sprinkle with the remaining cheese and cilantro. Scatter the jalapeños on top. Serve immediately or refrigerate until ready to serve or up to 2 hours.

Store leftovers in an airtight container in the refrigerator for up to 5 days.

Swap It: If you don't want to make pickled red onions for this salad, try swapping in a different pickle. You're really just looking for something acidic and crunchy to give this salad a little pop and contrast with the cheese, avocado, and dressing. Reach for a jar of dill pickles, chop up a few pepperoncini, or even throw in some Beet Pickled Turnips (page 213).

GREEN BEANS WITH FRIED LEMON, HOT HONEY, AND ALMONDS

SERVES 4 TO 6

Here's a crisp and lemony side dish that really lets green beans take the spotlight. This dish is beautiful in a haphazard way, and I like it because you can see the jumble of colours and textures that go into making it irresistible. It's a terrific companion to a simple piece of roasted fish, cold boiled potatoes drowned in a bit of vinaigrette, or even a quick Perfectly Poached Egg (page 69).

- 1 small yellow onion, thinly sliced
- 2 tablespoons (30 mL) olive oil, divided
- 1 pound (450 g) green beans, ends removed
- Pinch of salt
- 1 lemon, thinly sliced and seeds removed
- 1 tablespoon (15 mL) Everyday Vinegar (page 21)
- 1 tablespoon (15 mL) hot honey
- ½ cup (125 mL) roasted almonds, chopped

Place the onions in a small bowl and fill it with ice water. Set aside.

In a large skillet over high heat, warm 1 tablespoon (15 mL) of the olive oil until it starts to shimmer. Add the green beans. Cook over high heat for 2 to 3 minutes, stirring once or twice, until the beans are bright green but not wilted. Season with the salt. Use tongs to transfer the beans to a clean plate.

Add the remaining 1 tablespoon (15 mL) olive oil to the skillet (no need to wipe it) and heat until it starts to shimmer. Add the sliced lemon. Fry until the lemon softens, about 1 to 2 minutes. Turn off the heat. Whisk in the everyday vinegar and hot honey. Add the beans back into the hot skillet so that they warm through but do not continue cooking.

Transfer the beans, lemon, and all of the juices to a large platter. Drain the water from the bowl holding the onions. Scatter the onions overtop. Sprinkle everything with the almonds. Serve immediately.

Store leftovers in an airtight container in the refrigerator for up to 5 days.

SERVES 4 TO 6

BASIC BITTER SALAD

1 medium head of radicchio
¼ cup (60 mL) extra-virgin olive oil
¼ cup (60 mL) white or red wine vinegar
¼ cup (60 mL) chopped toasted pistachios
2 tablespoons (30 mL) pomegranate molasses

This is such a simple salad, consisting only of a crisp head of radicchio, oil, vinegar, pomegranate molasses, and pistachios. It is elegant in its simplicity and a wonderful partner for richer dishes like pan-roasted chicken thighs or even a platter of cured meats and cheeses. Use a knife and fork if you must, but this is a particularly good salad to eat with your hands on a hot day.

Cut the radicchio in half down the middle from top to bottom. Trim out the core and discard. Separate the leaves and lay about half on a medium platter.

In a small bowl, whisk together the olive oil and vinegar. Spoon about half the dressing over the radicchio. Arrange the remaining radicchio leaves overtop and drizzle with the remaining dressing. Sprinkle the chopped pistachios over everything, then drizzle it with the pomegranate molasses. Serve immediately.

Swap It: For something slightly less basic in the summer months, I like to thinly slice a handful of the freshest, deepest-burgundy cherries I can find and tuck them in between the leaves of radicchio for a burst of flavour and pleasure.

If you happen to be feeding a crowd, this salad responds very well to the introduction of other bitter lettuces, like a head of endive separated into leaves, or frisée, or both. Simply adjust the amount of dressing you make and the quantity of nuts and molasses you use accordingly.

BITTER IS BETTER

Bitter greens are one of my favourite ingredients, and a great way to add variety and interest to dishes. Along with sour, sweet, salty, and savoury (umami), bitter is one of the five basic tastes. Bitter greens, like endive, radicchio, and frisée, can really stand up to a lot of spice, acid, and even salt, so don't be afraid to dress them well. They are also wonderful paired with rich dishes, like a roast chicken or a big ol' slab of steak.

Aside from their rich and often complex flavour, bitter greens have the added benefit of kicking your digestive system into high gear. This is not a wellness cookbook, so I'm not going to do a deep dive into all the benefits, but basically once the flavour of bitterness hits your tongue, your primal brain, the one that is descended from hunter-gatherers who ate random bushberries, sends a message to your digestive tract because it thinks you may have eaten something poisonous and it wants to get everything moving as quickly as possible. This is useful knowledge, and I've made it a point to always include a dish or two centred on bitter greens any time I'm cooking a big meal or serving something particularly unctuous that needs a sharp counterpoint.

SERVES 4 TO 6

CHARRED RADICCHIO WITH WHIPPED HAZELNUT BUTTER, PLUMS, AND BACON

½ cup (125 mL) hazelnut butter (see Swap It)
½ cup (125 mL) cold water
Pinch of salt, plus more to taste
2 tablespoons (30 mL) olive oil
3 slices thick-cut bacon
2 medium heads radicchio, each cut into 6 wedges
2 tablespoons (30 mL) red wine vinegar
3 small red plums, pitted and torn into chunks
¼ cup (60 mL) chopped hazelnuts, toasted

Here is a warm salad comprised of many good flavours that you might not think to put next to each other. When combined, however, they come together with a magical sort of synergy and display a chaotic beauty. With creamy hazelnut butter, charred bitter radicchio, juicy red plums, and crisp, salty bacon all drizzled in a sharp red wine vinaigrette and topped with a fistful of crunchy toasted nuts, this is a dish that will hit every part of your palate and be the star of your next gathering. Serve it alongside something simple yet elegant, like seared scallops finished in butter and a splash of whatever wine you're drinking (I recommend a light fruity red like a gamay), or the best bread you can find, sliced thick and untoasted.

Place the hazelnut butter in a medium bowl. Slowly whisk in the cold water until it is fully incorporated and the hazelnut butter is pale and creamy. Season with a pinch of salt.

Line a plate with paper towels. Line a small sieve with a coffee filter and place it over a small bowl.

Place the olive oil and the bacon in a large cast-iron skillet over medium-high heat. Let the bacon render and sizzle, flipping occasionally, until crisp, 5 to 7 minutes. Use tongs to transfer the bacon to the prepared plate. Do not discard the oil in the skillet.

Increase the heat to high. Sprinkle the radicchio wedges with salt to taste and place them in the same skillet you used to cook the bacon. Sear the radicchio for about 1 minute on each cut side. You want the wedges to brown and caramelize slightly, but not completely wilt down. Transfer the radicchio to the plate with the bacon.

Carefully pour the oil from the skillet through the coffee filter to strain out any charred or crispy bits. Whisk the red wine vinegar into the warm oil to make a simple vinaigrette. Set aside.

Use a large spoon to dollop the hazelnut butter onto a large plate or platter. Arrange the radicchio on top. Tear the bacon into bite-sized chunks and scatter it overtop. Do the same with the plums. Drizzle the warm red wine vinaigrette all over. Top with the toasted hazelnuts. Serve immediately.

Swap It: Hazelnut butter is a lovely addition to any pantry. However, if you find yourself without, please don't run to the store for it or, worse, omit the nut butter component from this recipe as it really does add something special. Instead, use tahini in its place, and swap out the toasted hazelnuts for a few tablespoons of toasted sesame seeds.

SAUTEED RAPINI WITH BURRATA, LEMON, AND PISTACHIOS

SERVES 4 TO 6

Rapini has a flavour superpower that allows it to combine with other tastes instead of overpowering them. It helps carry the flavours of a dish forward so they hit all your tastebuds. This recipe makes full use of that superpower but goes a step further by adding a plump ball of burrata to the mix. Burrata has a thin skin that when pierced or sliced reveals oozy, creamy curds of stracciatella and brings a counterpoint to both the big flavours of lemon and chili and the crunchy textures of the rest of the dish. Serve this in proximity to Green Pasta with Lemon and Pecorino (page 144) or in collaboration with Braised Lamb Shanks with Butter Beans (page 162).

2 bunches rapini
3 tablespoons (45 mL) olive oil, more for drizzling
2 teaspoons (10 mL) salt, more to taste
Juice of 1 lemon
8 ounces (225 g) burrata cheese, drained
2 tablespoons (30 mL) hot honey
1 teaspoon (5 mL) ground red chilies (see Tip)
¼ cup (60 mL) pistachios, toasted and chopped

Trim the woody ends, about 2 inches (5 cm), off the bottom of the rapini and discard. Cut off the stems where they begin to branch into the leaves. Set the leaves aside.

In a large cast-iron skillet over high heat, warm the oil until it starts to shimmer. Add the rapini stems. Sprinkle with 2 teaspoons (10 mL) of salt. Stir so that they cook evenly for about 2 to 3 minutes, until they are bright green but still quite crisp. Add the leaves to the skillet. Cook for 1 to 2 minutes more, until the leaves have wilted and the stems are crisp-tender. Turn off the heat. Sprinkle the lemon juice overtop. Toss to evenly coat the rapini in the oil and lemon juice.

Transfer the rapini to a large plate or platter. Use your hands to tear the burrata open over the rapini. Drizzle everything with hot honey and some extra-virgin olive oil. Sprinkle with salt, to taste, followed by the red chilies and chopped pistachios. Serve warm.

Leftovers can be stored in an airtight container in the fridge for up to 5 days.

Tip: I prefer ground red chilies to chili flakes because they are subtler both in taste and in how they appear in a dish. You can buy ground red chilies in many forms, but you can also simply grind your own. To do so, use kitchen scissors to stem and seed your favourite dried chilies (I like guajillo). Toast the chilies for 2 to 3 minutes over medium-high heat in an unoiled cast-iron skillet until they darken and become fragrant. Then, blend them in a high-speed blender to the coarseness you want. You can store them in an airtight container for up to 6 months.

SERVES 4

ENDIVE, GRAPEFRUIT, AND FENNEL SALAD

2 small heads Belgian endive
1 bulb of fennel, thinly sliced
1 large red or Ruby Red grapefruit, peeled and sliced (see Swap It)
¼ cup (60 mL) pistachios, toasted and chopped
¼ cup (60 mL) extra-virgin olive oil
Hot honey, for drizzling

This is really more of an ingredient list than a recipe, but in case you haven't had the pleasure of trying the following list of things together before, I'm here to encourage you to get an icy cold plate and perhaps an Aperol spritz, and to lay out the most perfect combination of sweet, sour, bitter, and even liquorice-y flavours, covered in good olive oil and crunchy green pistachios.

Separate the leaves of the endive and trim out any tough core bits. Arrange the endive, fennel, and grapefruit on a large plate or platter. Top with the pistachios and drizzle with the olive oil and hot honey. Serve immediately.

Store leftovers in an airtight container in the fridge for up to 2 days.

Swap It: Any sweet citrus fruit will work here—try oranges, mandarins, or even pomelo!

CRUNCHY CELERY CAESAR WITH TONNATO AND HAZELNUTS

SERVES 4

Whenever I explain tonnato—essentially a mayonnaise made out of good-quality tinned tuna—to my cooking class students, I get a few raised eyebrows at the thought of eating puréed fish. But once I reframe tonnato as a more intense Caesar dressing, made using tuna instead of anchovies, I'm typically able to get the skeptics on board.

This recipe highlights just how Caesar-adjacent tonnato is. With a bit of extra garlic and some Caesar musts like lemon, cheese, black pepper, and a good shower of crunchy bread bits, this dish holds universal appeal and has the sort of casual gravitas that's impressive. Pair it with Steak Night Steak (page 203) for a cool, crunchy counterpoint to the hot, juicy, slightly spicy steak, or keep it simple and serve it next to some charred bread and a tin of butter beans drizzled in good olive oil.

½ cup (125 mL) Tonnato (page 52)
1 clove garlic, finely grated
Juice of 1 lemon
1 medium bunch celery, thinly sliced
½ cup (125 mL) hazelnuts, toasted and lightly chopped
¼ cup (60 mL) Crunchy Bread Bits (page 140)
4 ounces (115 g) pecorino cheese, shaved
½ Cured Egg Yolk (page 77)
Fresh cracked black pepper

In a medium bowl, whisk together the tonnato, garlic, and lemon juice. Add the celery. Toss well to combine. Transfer the celery to a medium platter. Top with the hazelnuts, crunchy bread bits, and pecorino cheese. Finely grate about ½ of a cured egg yolk on top. Finish with lots of fresh cracked black pepper. Serve immediately.

Store leftovers in an airtight container in the fridge for up to 2 days.

SERVES 4

CREAMED GREENS AND CRUNCHY BREAD BITS

3 bunches curly kale, Swiss chard, or other greens
2 tablespoons (30 mL) olive oil
Pinch of ground red chilies
Salt and fresh cracked black pepper
1 cup (250 mL) heavy (35%) cream
¾ cup (175 mL) labneh or plain Greek yogurt
½ cup (125 mL) finely grated pecorino cheese
½ cup (125 mL) Crunchy Bread Bits (page 140)

I love heartier greens like kale and chard because they hold up well to some gentle cookery and a good amount of creamy dairy. With this recipe, you can use whatever greens you've got on hand, or even things like beet greens and the stiff, pale leaves that sometimes come wrapped around the edges of your cauliflower. Adding labneh and pecorino in addition to heavy cream tempers the richness of this dish, and the Crunchy Bread Bits (page 140) add a little contrast and excitement without much effort or expense.

Preheat the oven to 475°F (240°C).

Rinse the greens and remove the stems. Cut the stems into 2-inch (5 cm) pieces and set aside. Tear the leaves into bite-sized pieces.

Warm the olive oil in a large cast-iron skillet over high heat. Once it shimmers, add the stems and cook for 2 to 3 minutes, stirring vigorously to prevent browning, until they are tender. Add the leaves and chilies, and season with salt and pepper to taste. Cook another 1 to 2 minutes until the greens wilt down. Pour in the cream. Continue cooking until the cream has thickened and reduced by half. Remove the skillet from the heat. Stir in the labneh and cheese.

Transfer the greens to a medium ovenproof dish. Top with the crunchy bread bits. Bake for 10 to 12 minutes, until the top is browned and the greens are bubbling. Let stand for about 5 minutes and serve.

Store leftovers in an airtight container in the refrigerator for up to 5 days.

Swap It: Make this gluten-free by leaving out the bread heel, doubling the tahini, and garnishing with Green Crunch Sauce (page 30) instead of herbs and bread bits.

GARLICKY EGGPLANT WITH SESAME ROMESCO AND HERBS

SERVES 2 TO 4

This recipe consists of tender, garlicky roasted eggplant in a puddle of romesco sauce, with lots of herby, crunchy stuff on top. There is so much flavour and texture to enjoy here and not a lot of active prep time.

Traditional romesco sauce is typically made with almonds or even occasionally pine nuts, but in order to keep costs down while still getting the same effect, I like to use tahini. Tahini adds a bit of richness and body to this sauce as well as just a little bitterness, which offsets the sweet peppers and garlic

Eggplant

1 large eggplant
2 tablespoons (30 mL) + 1 teaspoon (5 mL) salt
¼ cup (60 mL) olive oil
2 cloves garlic

Romesco Sauce

¼ cup (60 mL) + 2 tablespoons (30 mL) olive oil
2 red bell peppers, roughly chopped, or 1 jar (16 ounces/475 mL) roasted red peppers, drained and roughly chopped
1 shallot or small yellow onion, roughly chopped
2 cloves garlic
1 bread heel, coarsely chopped
Pinch of ground red chilies
Pinch of salt
2 tablespoons (30 mL) tahini
1 tablespoon (15 mL) red wine vinegar or Everyday Vinegar (page 21)

To serve

Fresh herbs such as flat-leaf parsley, mint, or basil, roughly chopped, to garnish
Handful of Crunchy Bread Bits (page 140)
Extra-virgin olive oil, for drizzling

Make the Eggplant: Preheat the oven to 425°F (220°C).

Holding the eggplant by the tip, with its base on a cutting board, slice off just enough of one side so that it will lie flat in a baking dish. Transfer the eggplant to your non-dominant hand, with the cut side in your palm. Use a Y-peeler to remove the remaining skin from the non-cut side of the eggplant. Place the eggplant on the cutting board and score the exposed flesh in a cross-hatch pattern using a sharp paring knife. Fill a medium bowl with lukewarm water and whisk in 2 tablespoons (30 mL) of the salt, until dissolved. Place the eggplant in the salty water and let it brine for 20 minutes at room temperature. Remove the eggplant and discard the brine. Pat the eggplant dry with paper towels.

In a small bowl, mix together the olive oil, garlic, and the remaining 1 teaspoon (5 mL) salt. Rub the mixture all over the eggplant, making sure it gets into the cross-hatched flesh. Place the eggplant in a medium ovenproof dish. Roast for about 1 hour, until the eggplant is tender all the way through but still holds its shape.

Make the Romesco Sauce: Warm 2 tablespoons (30 mL) of the olive oil in a large skillet over high heat. Add the peppers, onion, garlic, and bread. Season with the chilies and a big pinch of salt. Cook for 5 to 7 minutes, stirring so that the vegetables soften and the bread gets a bit toasty. Transfer everything to a high-powered blender. Add the tahini and vinegar. Pulse to combine. With the blender running on high speed, slowly stream in the remaining ¼ cup (60 mL) olive oil until fully combined and smooth.

To serve: Use a big spoon to dollop and schmear the romesco into an oval on a similarly shaped platter. Place the warm eggplant on top. Scatter the herbs and bread bits overtop. Drizzle with olive oil. Serve immediately.

Store leftovers in an airtight container in the fridge for up to 5 days.

SERVES 4

SPICY ROASTED CAULIFLOWER OVER WHIPPED TAHINI

1 head of cauliflower, broken into bite-sized florets
¼ cup (60 mL) olive oil
Pinch of salt
¼ cup (60 mL) Honey Harissa (page 25), more to serve
1 cup (250 mL) or so Whipped Tahini (page 18)
Toasted sesame seeds, to garnish
Squeeze of lemon (optional)

Raw cauliflower is fine, but cauliflower that's been rubbed all over with oil and salt and placed in a hot oven until it's developed a charred, nutty flavour and lots of little crispy bits is in a different league. At that point, you don't need to do too much to it, but this dish levels up with Honey Harissa (page 25), creamy Whipped Tahini (page 18), and a smattering of crunchy toasted sesame seeds.

Preheat the oven to 500°F (260°C). Line a medium baking sheet with parchment paper.

Place the cauliflower florets in a medium bowl. Drizzle with olive oil and a big pinch of salt. Toss until the cauliflower is evenly coated. Spread it out on the prepared baking sheet. Roast until the outsides have gone crispy and the inside is tender, about 12 to 15 minutes. Return the cauliflower to the bowl. Add ¼ cup of the honey harissa. Toss until evenly coated.

To serve, use a large spoon to dollop and then schmear the tahini into a roughly oval shape on a large platter. Mound the cauliflower on top. Drizzle it with a bit more honey harissa and sprinkle it with the sesame seeds. Squeeze some lemon juice on top (if using). Serve warm.

Store leftovers in an airtight container in the fridge for up to 5 days. If you're looking for a fast lunch or an easy dinner, leftovers of this dish make a particularly good filling for a warm pita alongside some pickles and fresh greens.

CHARRED CABBAGE WITH KIELBASA VINAIGRETTE

SERVES 4 TO 6

This is a wonderful recipe to keep in your back pocket for those moments when you need to conjure something delicious for family and friends on short notice. The kielbasa is slashed and pan-roasted so that its juices, when combined with a dash of vinegar and a dollop each of honey and Dijon, become a salty, smoky vinaigrette. The vinaigrette is then poured all over a head of nutty roasted cabbage, creamy labneh, and lightly pickled red onions. A handful of rye bread crumbs really brings everything together. The result is a dish that feels at once familiar and luxurious.

Cabbage
1 small Savoy cabbage
¼ cup (60 mL) olive oil
2 teaspoons (10 mL) salt

Kielbasa Vinaigrette
½ pound (225 g) kielbasa sausage
¼ cup (60 mL) olive oil, divided
¼ cup (60 mL) white vinegar
1 tablespoon (15 mL) Dijon mustard
1 tablespoon (15 mL) pure liquid honey

Quick-Pickled Red Onions
½ red onion, thinly sliced
Pinch of salt
Pinch of sugar
1 tablespoon (15 mL) white vinegar

To serve
½ cup (125 mL) full-fat sour cream or labneh
1 tablespoon (15 mL) caraway seeds
2 slices dark rye bread, toasted and chopped fine
Handful of fresh dill, lightly chopped
Fresh cracked black pepper
Juice of ½ lemon (optional)

Roast the Cabbage: Preheat the oven to 500°F (260°C). Line a large baking sheet with parchment paper.

Keeping the core of the cabbage intact, slice it into thin wedges. Place the cabbage wedges in a large bowl. Add the olive oil and salt. Toss to coat the cabbage.

Spread out the cabbage wedges on the prepared baking sheet. Roast for 15 minutes. Remove the baking sheet from the oven and flip the wedges. Return the cabbage to the oven and bake for another 10 minutes, until lightly charred on both sides.

Make the Kielbasa Vinaigrette: Cut the kielbasa into 2-inch (5 cm) lengths. Score each length 5 or 6 times on the bias, cutting two-thirds of the way through.

Warm 2 tablespoons (30 mL) of the olive oil in a large skillet over high heat. Add the kielbasa and let brown for 3 to 4 minutes. Whisk in the vinegar, mustard, honey, and the remaining 2 tablespoons (30 mL) olive oil. Remove from the heat.

Prepare the Quick-Pickled Red Onions: In a small bowl, massage the onions with the salt and sugar so that they soften. Add the vinegar. Toss to combine.

To serve: Arrange the cabbage on a large platter. Add the sour cream in dollops. Spoon the kielbasa vinaigrette over everything. Drain any excess liquid from the onions and scatter them on top. Sprinkle the caraway seeds, rye crumbs, and dill over everything. Top with fresh cracked black pepper to taste and lemon juice (if using). Serve immediately.

Store leftovers in an airtight container in the fridge for up to 5 days.

PULL FROM THE PANTRY

I WROTE THIS CHAPTER BECAUSE I MEET a lot of people who feel as though they should be shopping at farmers' markets and boutique grocers to eat well. While that is one way to live, it's not the only way, and for many of us—people who are on a budget, people who don't have as much time as we'd like to shop, people who experience winter storms—there's no shame in grabbing a can, a jar, or a bag of something and putting it to work in your kitchen.

A real cornerstone of my kitchen is a pantry loaded up with my favourites—and by pantry I mean both my haphazard dry goods cupboard and my freezer, which is stashed with all manner of frozen fruits, vegetables, seeds, and things like bread heels and cheese rinds that have been packed in cloudy-looking zip-top bags.

A full pantry ensures that you are prepared to knock together a meal that is quick and delicious. You'll find you are the hero of your own gustatory challenge when you rifle around a bit, discover a bag of pasta and a tin of tuna behind a half-eaten bag of salt and vinegar chips, and set about making Creamy Pasta with Peas, Tuna, and Salt and Vinegar Chips (page 136), or perhaps you pop open a jar of roasted red peppers, rummage around in your own murky bag of bread heels, and create a cozy, comforting, and oh-so-quick bowl of Red Pepper Soup with Limey Yogurt and Basil Oil (page 131).

CHILLED BUTTERMILK PEA SOUP WITH STRAWBERRY TOAST

SERVES 4 TO 6

Cold soup on a hot day is one of my favourite things in the warmer months. This version, which combines frozen peas and tangy buttermilk, comes together in moments. Peas and strawberries are a classic pairing, and the creamy labneh and crunchy toast add both texture and interest. This is a great starter for your next dinner party, since it is more or less effortless but still impressive.

Pea Soup

3 cups (750 mL) buttermilk (see Tip)
1 cup (250 mL) water
4 cups (1 L) frozen peas, rinsed to remove any chunks of frost or ice
Handful of fresh basil
Pinch of salt
1 tablespoon (15 mL) pure liquid honey

Strawberry Toast

¼ cup (60 mL) strawberry jam
2 tablespoons (30 mL) white vinegar
½ cup (125 mL) labneh, ricotta, or plain Greek yogurt
4 to 6 thin slices baguette, toasted
Fresh cracked black pepper
Basil Oil (page 29), to serve

Place 4 to 6 bowls in the freezer to chill, depending on how many people you plan to serve.

Make the Pea Soup: Place the buttermilk, water, frozen peas, basil, salt, and honey in a high-speed blender. Purée until smooth. Place the soup in the fridge to stay cold.

Make the Strawberry Toast: In a small bowl, stir together the jam and vinegar. Spread the labneh on the toasts and top with the jam mixture and fresh cracked black pepper to taste.

Divide the soup among the chilled bowls. Drizzle each serving with basil oil. Balance a piece of strawberry toast on the edge of each bowl and serve immediately.

Store leftover soup in an airtight container in the fridge for up to 5 days.

Tip: Using 3 cups (750 mL) of buttermilk will leave you with 1 cup (250 mL) left in the carton. Don't worry! Head to page 257 and make Maple Buttermilk Panna Cotta with Cinnamon Toast Crumbles and Blueberries to use it all up.

SERVES 4 TO 6

PEPPERONCINI POTATO SALAD WITH FETA AND CILANTRO

1½ pounds (675 g) baby potatoes
4 ounces (115 g) feta, crumbled, plus 1 tablespoon (15 mL) brine
1 cup (250 mL) pepperoncini, chopped, plus 1 tablespoon (15 mL) brine
2 tablespoons (30 mL) labneh or plain Greek yogurt
2 to 3 scallions, chopped
Pinch of ground cumin
Handful of fresh cilantro, chopped
Salt

As far as I know, there are only two ways a potato salad can go: it can be creamy, or it can be dressed with a vinaigrette. Although different, both have their merits. This is a creamy potato salad, but because of the briny feta, tangy yogurt, and spicy-sharp pepperoncini, it manages to pack a lot more flavour than your average mayonnaise-dressed version. It's a fine partner for something like Steak Night Steak (page 203) but can also round out a plate of Cod Cakes with Dilly Mayo (page 209) or whatever you're tossing on the grill for an impromptu barbecue.

Place the potatoes in a medium saucepan of cold, salted water over high heat (see Tip). Make sure they have ample room to bob around and they aren't jammed in there shoulder to shoulder. Once the water comes to a boil, reduce the heat to just above a simmer. Cook the potatoes at a gentle bubble for 5 to 7 minutes, until they are easily pierced with a paring knife. Drain the liquid.

Transfer the potatoes to a medium bowl. Use a big spoon to smash them up a bit. This will help them absorb all the good flavours you're going to add to them. Toss the potatoes to help release steam and to ensure they don't keep cooking in the bowl.

Add the feta and brine, pepperoncini and brine, labneh, scallions, cumin, and cilantro, then season to taste with salt. Toss until the potatoes are evenly coated. Serve warm, at ambient temperature, or cold.

Store leftovers in an airtight container in the fridge for up to 5 days. I also recommend stuffing them into a pita.

Tip: You should always start your potatoes in cold water so that they cook evenly. If you place them in boiling water, the outsides will cook before the insides. This will result in potatoes that are both gluey and crunchy at the same time.

Tip: Any time you add something acidic like lemon juice or vinegar to cooked green vegetables, such as peas, broccoli, or asparagus, do it immediately before serving to prevent them from going brown.

RICOTTA AND PEA STUFFED CHEESE PUFFS

SERVES 7 AS A STARTER

A classic French hors d'oeuvre called a gougère, which is essentially a cheese puff. Usually, gougères are bite-sized, but here I've made them large enough to stuff. The combination of warm, golden puff, creamy ricotta, and bright green peas feels really high-end, but you'll be surprised by how easy it is to make.

Cheese Puffs
1 cup (250 mL) water
½ cup (125 mL) unsalted butter, cubed
Pinch of salt
Pinch of sugar
1 cup (250 mL) all-purpose flour
4 to 5 eggs
1 cup (250 mL) grated Gruyère cheese

Ricotta Filling
2 cups (500 mL) ricotta
1 tablespoon (15 mL) olive oil
Juice of ½ lemon
Handful of fresh chives, chopped
Pinch of ground red chilies
Salt and pepper

Peas
2 tablespoons (30 mL) unsalted butter
1 cup (250 mL) frozen peas
Salt and pepper
Juice of ½ lemon
Handful of fresh chives, chopped

To serve (optional)
Pea shoots or other fresh herbs, such as basil or mint
Basil oil, for drizzling

Make the Cheese Puffs: Preheat the oven to 400°F (200°C). Line a baking sheet with parchment paper.

Place the water in a medium saucepan over high heat. Stir in the butter, salt, and sugar, until the butter melts and the sugar dissolves. Add the flour. Using a wooden spoon, stir briskly to keep the flour from sticking to the bottom of the pot as it combines with the water to form a dough. Reduce the heat to medium-high. Continue stirring until the dough becomes quite stiff, about 2 to 3 minutes. Remove the saucepan from the heat. Using the wooden spoon, beat in the eggs, one at a time, until they are fully absorbed. The dough should be shiny and thick enough to hold its shape. If you are using large or extra-large eggs, 4 should be enough, but you may need to add one additional egg or even just the yolk if they are on the smaller side and your dough is still a bit stiff. Stir in the grated cheese, until combined.

Using a pastry brush dipped in water, moisten the parchment on the baking sheet. This will help the puffs rise. Divide the dough into 7 equal portions, spacing them out on the tray so they have room to expand. Bake for 20 to 25 minutes, until nicely puffed and golden brown. Use a toothpick to poke a small hole in the side of each puff so that the steam can escape. Set the puffs on a rack to cool.

Make the Ricotta Filling: In a medium bowl, combine the ricotta, olive oil, lemon juice, chives, and chilies. Season with salt and pepper to taste and mix well.

Make the Peas: In a large skillet over medium-high heat, melt the butter. Add the peas. Cook for 3 to 4 minutes, stirring frequently, until they are hot through and bright green. Season with salt and pepper to taste. Just before serving, add the lemon juice and chives (see Tip). Stir to combine.

Assemble the dish: Use a serrated knife to slice each puff like you would a sandwich bun, leaving enough puff to act as a hinge on one side. Stuff the puffs by dividing the ricotta evenly among them, then spooning the peas overtop. Sprinkle a few pea shoots on top of the peas and drizzle them with basil oil (if using). Close the lid of each puff and serve immediately.

SERVES 4

FAST FRENCH ONION SOUP WITH CRISPY GRUYÈRE

- 2 tablespoons (30 mL) olive oil
- 8 medium yellow onions, thinly sliced
- 1 teaspoon (5 mL) sugar
- 2 pinches salt, more to taste
- Pinch of baking soda
- 5 sprigs fresh thyme, plus more for the crispy Gruyère
- 2 cups (500 mL) light- or medium-bodied dry red wine, like gamay or pinot noir
- 1 tablespoon (15 mL) red wine vinegar or Everyday Vinegar (page 21), more to taste
- 6 cups (1.5 L) low-sodium beef broth
- 2 cups (500 mL) grated Gruyère, Swiss, or Emmenthal cheese, divided
- Fresh cracked black pepper

This recipe is inspired by my husband, Oscar, who often begins musing mid-afternoon about what he would like for dinner, with no sense of how long a dish might actually take to make. This recipe cuts the cooking time of traditional French onion soup from well over an hour (some people will even say several hours) down to about 30 minutes. Using baking soda to help caramelize the onions quickly and then cooking them hot and hard with red wine results in a rich base for the broth. While I am rarely one to eschew toast, skipping the carbs here and going all in on a big disk of fried cheese is a really wonderful twist.

In a large skillet over high heat, warm the olive oil until it starts to shimmer. Add the onions, sugar, and 1 pinch of salt. Let the onions brown, but not burn, for 4 to 5 minutes over high heat, stirring once or twice. Add the baking soda. Toss so that the baking soda is evenly distributed. Cook for another 5 to 10 minutes, until the onions have browned.

Tie together the thyme sprigs using butcher's twine. Still working over high heat, add the red wine, vinegar, and thyme to the skillet. Cook until the mixture has reduced by half. Add the beef broth, plus another pinch of salt. Reduce the heat to a low simmer and continue cooking for 15 to 20 minutes, until the flavours have melded and the onions are jammy and tender. Check the seasoning and add more salt if desired.

Meanwhile, place a medium cast-iron skillet over medium-high heat. Sprinkle about ½ cup (125 mL) of the cheese into the skillet and allow it to melt, then bubble, until the bottom looks golden and brown, 2 to 3 minutes. Add a sprinkle of fresh thyme leaves and a few cracks of black pepper (see Tip). Flip the cheese using a perforated spatula. Cook for another 30 seconds. Transfer the crispy Gruyère to a wire rack to cool slightly. Repeat 3 more times for a total of 4 pieces of crispy cheese.

To serve, use a pair of tongs to fish the thyme bundle out of the soup. Discard. Taste the soup and add additional salt to taste and another splash of vinegar, if desired. Divide the soup into 4 bowls. Top each one with a piece of crispy Gruyère and a few more cracks of black pepper. Serve immediately.

Store leftover soup in an airtight container in the fridge for up to 5 days.

Tip: Not required, but if I'm really going for it, I will sprinkle crispy onions into the melting Gruyère for an extra hit of crunch and some extra onion flavour.

RED PEPPER SOUP WITH LIMEY YOGURT AND BASIL OIL

SERVES 4 TO 6

A few jars of roasted red peppers are a must for my pantry. They are great puréed into sauces and soups, particularly in the winter months, when fresh peppers are either hard to find or expensive (see Tip). This soup uses one whole jar of roasted red peppers and gives them a flavour boost with a bit of Red Pepper Butter (page 17). Critical to any puréed soup is a smooth, silky texture, and here that is achieved with the addition of a good amount of olive oil, as well as some toasted bread, which adds a bit of body. A simple lime yogurt brings acidity and a little visual interest. The result is a very fast and very pretty soup.

Red Pepper Soup

6 tablespoons (90 mL) olive oil, divided
2 jars (16 ounces/475 mL each) roasted red peppers, drained
1 small yellow onion, sliced
2 cloves garlic
Pinch of salt, more to taste
2 tablespoons (30 mL) Red Pepper Butter (page 17) or tomato paste
Pinch of sugar (optional)
4 cups (1 L) water
2 slices bread or bread heels, toasted

Limey Yogurt

¼ cup (60 mL) plain Greek yogurt or labneh
Juice of ½ lime
1 tablespoon (15 mL) water, more if needed

To serve

Basil Oil (page 29), for drizzling
Fresh cracked black pepper

Make the Red Pepper Soup: In a large saucepan over high heat, warm 2 tablespoons (30 mL) of the olive oil until it starts to shimmer. Add the peppers, onion, garlic, and a large pinch of salt. Cook for 2 to 3 minutes, until the onions soften, stirring often so that they do not brown. Reduce the heat to medium. Add the red pepper butter. Cook for 1 minute. Add the pinch of sugar (if using). Stir to combine. Add the water to the mixture. Increase the heat to high and bring the soup to a boil, then reduce the heat to a simmer and cook for 15 minutes. Remove the saucepan from the heat.

Tear the toast into bite-sized chunks. Place about half of the toast chunks in a high-speed blender. Add about half of the hot soup. Purée until smooth. With the blender running, pour in about 2 tablespoons (30 mL) of the olive oil until combined. Transfer the soup to a large saucepan to keep warm. Repeat the process with the remaining soup, toast, and olive oil. Mix the soup together and add salt to taste.

Make the Limey Yogurt: In a small bowl, whisk together the yogurt, lime juice, and water. If the yogurt is still quite thick, add another 1 tablespoon (15 mL) of water. The resulting mixture should be the consistency of heavy cream.

To serve: Divide the soup among 4 to 6 bowls. Spoon a little limey yogurt on top of each. Drizzle each serving with basil oil and add a few cracks of black pepper.

Store leftovers in an airtight container in the fridge for up to 5 days.

Tip: If you're looking for more ways to incorporate roasted red peppers into your cooking, they are perfect thinly sliced and tossed into a pasta salad with some tinned artichokes and a fistful of arugula, or perhaps chopped and sprinkled on a pizza, or even layered on top of thickly spread labneh or cream cheese on a hunk of baguette.

SERVES 4 TO 5

MELTY CHEESE AND PEPPERONCINI PULL-APART ROLLS

- 12 slider-size Hawaiian rolls or dinner rolls
- ¼ cup (60 mL) unsalted butter, melted
- 2 cups (500 mL) grated provolone, Swiss, or mozzarella cheese
- 1 cup (250 mL) pepperoncini, roughly chopped

Pepperoncini are a tremendously useful pantry staple. They are spicy, but not too spicy, crunchy, green, and come in a zippy brine that can be used to flavour dressings, soups, sauces, salads, and spreads. This recipe is incredibly easy and always a huge hit. The buns get toasty, the cheese gets melty and oozy, and the pepperoncini hold on to just the right amount of spicy crunchy goodness. Serve these alongside a homemade or good-quality tinned soup, or throw them together for your next potluck or games night.

Preheat the oven to 350°F (180°C). Line a baking sheet with parchment paper.

Use a serrated knife to slice the tops off the buns. Brush the cut side of the bottoms with about half of the melted butter. Sprinkle about half of the cheese over the butter, then top with the pepperoncini and the remaining cheese. Place the tops of the buns over the cheese. Brush with the remaining butter. Bake for 15 to 18 minutes, until the buns are toasty and the cheese is melty. Serve immediately.

HERBY FETA ORZO

SERVES 4 TO 6

This is an easy pasta you can make to round out a meal or as a side to some leftovers you're trying to stretch, like Braised Lamb Shanks with Butter Beans (page 162), for instance. This recipe will take you about as long to make as the pasta takes to cook and can be eaten warm, at ambient temperature, or cold. Use whatever combination of herbs you have—there is no need to spend time mincing them, since they are best when they are just roughly torn and add colour, texture, and freshness in an effortless way.

1 pound (450 g) orzo pasta
Olive oil, for drizzling
1 cup (250 mL) crumbled feta, more to garnish
½ cup (125 mL) Honey Harissa (page 25, see Swap It)
1 cup (250 mL) torn fresh herbs and greens, such as mint, basil, flat-leaf parsley, dill, or arugula

Cook the orzo according to the package instructions. Drain thoroughly and place the pasta in a large bowl. Drizzle with olive oil. Toss to coat evenly. Add the feta and honey harissa. Toss to combine. The pasta can be refrigerated until ready to serve.

Before serving, stir the orzo to break up any clumps. Gently fold in the herbs. Sprinkle a bit of feta on top and drizzle with olive oil.

Store leftovers in an airtight container in the fridge for up to 5 days.

Swap It: You can also make this dish using ½ cup (125 mL) of Red Pepper Butter (page 17) in place of the Honey Harissa.

SERVES 4 TO 6

CREAMY PASTA WITH PEAS, TUNA, AND SALT AND VINEGAR CHIPS

1 pound (450 g) cavatappi, linguini, or orecchiette pasta
Olive oil, for drizzling
2 cups (500 mL) frozen peas
3 cans (2.8 ounces/80 g each) tuna packed in olive oil, drained
2 cups (500 mL) sour cream or labneh
Juice of ½ lemon
1 cup (125 mL) grated pecorino cheese, more for garnish
Salt
Fresh cracked black pepper
Handful of fresh dill, chopped
1 cup (250 mL) salt and vinegar chips, crushed

This recipe for a creamy tuna- and pea-studded pasta smothered in salty chips and fresh dill has universal appeal. Kids love it because chips are delicious, adults can tap into the familiar flavour profile of a tuna noodle casserole, and I appreciate it because it takes minimal effort and time to put together.

Bring a large saucepan of salted water to a rolling boil over high heat. Cook the pasta according to package instructions. Just before draining, remove 1 cup (250 mL) of the pasta water and set aside. Drain the pasta. Drizzle with some olive oil to keep it from sticking together.

Return the empty saucepan to the stove over high heat. Add the reserved pasta water and peas. Cook for 1 to 2 minutes, or until the peas are bright green and warmed through. Add the tuna, sour cream, lemon juice, and 1 cup (250 mL) of the pecorino cheese. Stir to combine. Add the pasta and toss to coat it evenly with the sauce. Season with salt to taste.

Divide the pasta into bowls. Top each serving with cracked black pepper to taste, chopped dill, more pecorino cheese, and a handful of crushed salt and vinegar chips.

Leftover pasta can be stored in an airtight container in the fridge, ungarnished, for up to 5 days.

HOW TO MAKE SOMETHING OUT OF NOTHING

If you visit my kitchen, you'll find jars and bags and containers holding items that might typically be discarded, like bread heels and cheese rinds, but that are actually things I'm *saving* because they are useful for adding flavour at no extra cost. Who doesn't love that? Next time you finish a jar of pickles, don't be so quick to toss the pickle juice! Read on and you may be surprised by all of the amazing ways you can use things that normally end up in the bin.

DILL PICKLE JUICE

- Boil it and pour it over a jar packed with fresh-cut veggies like cucumbers, carrots, celery, radishes, or turnips to make quick pickles.
- Use it to poach your Dill Pickle Poached Cod with Scallion Sauce (page 157).
- Soak thinly sliced white onions in it to make a great topping for burgers, tacos, or nachos.
- Mix 2 tablespoons (30 mL) of it into ½ cup (125 mL) mayonnaise with a handful of herbs or chopped-up pickles to make a tartar-y sauce.
- Use it in lieu of vinegar in salad and coleslaw dressings.
- Splash it over grilled pork chops, or mix it with a a tablespoon of butter and toss your baked chicken wings in it.

PICKLED BEET JUICE

- Toss thinly sliced onions in it for a pretty pink onion garnish loaded with flavour.
- Place soft- or hard-boiled eggs in a jar of pickled beet juice for about 20 minutes for deliciously pink and pickle-y eggs.
- Save the juice for your next batch of beet borscht: it will add both flavour and acidity.

FETA BRINE

- Marinate chicken in it for 1 to 2 hours before grilling or roasting for tender, seasoned chicken that is perfect for stuffing in a pita or slicing and adding to a chopped salad of cucumbers and tomatoes.
- Use it to replace some of the vinegar in your favourite salad dressing recipe: it's particularly well suited to Greek salads.
- Purée your feta with a couple of tablespoons each of feta brine and the dairy of your choice, for example yogurt, labneh, or heavy (35%) cream, and then use it as a sandwich spread or spoon it into a dish, drizzle it all with hot honey, and use it as a dip for fresh veggies or crunchy seed crackers.

VEGETABLE SCRAPS

- Freeze vegetable trimmings from non-starchy vegetables like onions, carrots, celery, tomatoes, zucchini, and fennel in a zip-top bag and add to your Chicken Broth (page 220). Or, if you've accumulated enough, use them to make vegetable broth.

STALE BREAD HEELS

- Toast them lightly and purée them into soups, like Red Pepper Soup with Limey Yogurt and Basil Oil (page 131), or sauces, such as Garlicky Eggplant with Sesame Romesco and Herbs (page 113).
- Grate them on a box grater and use them in One-Pot Meatballs and Spaghetti (page 161).
- Roughly chop them, toss them with olive oil, and then bake or pan-fry them until they're golden brown. Chop them again and—voilà!—you have Crunchy Bread Bits, which are somewhere between a crouton and a bread crumb and work as a crunchy garnish on soups, pastas, salads, and dishes like Braised Lamb Shanks with Butter Beans (page 162).
- Finely grind them in a high-speed blender or food processor and use the bread crumbs when making Cod Cakes with Dilly Mayo (page 209) or Crispy Pork Salad with Pickles, Herbs, and Spicy Mayo (page 191).

CHEESE ENDS

- Slip rinds into soups, stews, pots of beans, and pasta sauces for added flavour and richness.
- Freeze cheese rinds in a zip-top bag and use them to calm teething babies.
- Freeze the last bits of cheese from a cheese board in a zip-top bag and when you have enough, thaw them and make Beer Cheese (page 56).

BACON FAT AND SCHMALTZ

- Roast vegetables in it, especially hearty root vegetables like carrots, parsnips, and squash.
- Use it in lieu of butter when you make Chicken and Dumplings (page 223).
- Use it to replace some or all of the oil in your salad dressings for an added flavour boost.

CHEESY RED PEPPER PASTA WITH CRUNCHY BREAD BITS

SERVES 1 TO 2

This is the ideal weeknight pasta for me. It takes less than ten minutes to put together, assuming you have some Red Pepper Butter (page 17) handy, and is beyond delicious. With all its saucy, cheesy, carb-y crunch, it is perfect for when hanger hits. This recipe is easily doubled or tripled, and it responds well to additions like a handful of thinly sliced green Castelvetrano olives or a smattering of chopped herbs, which you can toss in at the end.

4 ounces (115 g) spaghetti or other pasta
½ cup (125 mL) Red Pepper Butter (page 17)
Salt
½ cup (125 mL) grated mozzarella cheese
Crunchy Bread Bits (page 140), to serve

Bring a large saucepan of salted water to a rolling boil over high heat. Cook the pasta for about 2 minutes less than the package recommends. Scoop out and reserve ½ cup (125 mL) of the pasta water. Drain the pasta.

Turn off the heat and return the empty saucepan to the burner. Add the reserved pasta water and the red pepper butter. Whisk together over the residual heat to form a sauce. Add the pasta. Continue cooking over the residual heat for 2 minutes, tossing all the while to coat the pasta in the sauce. Season with salt to taste. Stir in the mozzarella until it melts.

Divide the pasta among bowls. Sprinkle crunchy bread bits (page 140) on top. Serve immediately.

Store leftovers in an airtight container in the fridge for up to 5 days.

SERVES 4

GREEN PASTA WITH LEMON AND PECORINO

1 pound (450 g) paccheri or other pasta
2 tablespoons (30 mL) olive oil, more for drizzling
2 cups (500 mL) frozen broccoli florets
2 cloves garlic
1 cup (250 mL) vegetable broth or chicken broth or water
4 cups (1 L) fresh or frozen baby spinach
Handful of fresh basil, plus more to garnish
½ cup (125 mL) heavy (35%) cream or labneh
Salt
Juice of 1 lemon
½ cup (125 mL) finely grated pecorino or Parmesan cheese, more to serve
Fresh cracked black pepper
Basil Oil (page 29), for drizzling

So many of my recipes are inspired by my family and what I often consider to be our specific—but also somehow relatable—needs. One of those needs is to get everyone to eat more vegetables. What better way to get the whole family on board with frozen broccoli and a few fistfuls of spinach than to combine them with fresh basil, add a bit of broth and cream, and then purée them into a silky sauce with lemon and pecorino? We love this green pasta sauce smothered all over big, soft pasta noodles, and whether you're cooking it or eating it or both, I think you will too!

Bring a large saucepan of salted water to a rolling boil over high heat. Cook the pasta for about 2 minutes less than the package recommends. Scoop out and reserve ½ cup (125 mL) of the pasta water. Drain the pasta. Drizzle it with olive oil and toss so that it doesn't stick together.

Return the empty saucepan to the burner and turn the heat up to high. Add the olive oil and broccoli. Cook for 2 minutes, stirring occasionally, until the broccoli turns bright green. Add the garlic cloves. Cook for 1 minute. Add the broth and bring to a boil. Add the spinach. Stir to wilt the spinach. Turn off the heat.

Using a slotted spoon, transfer the broccoli, garlic, and spinach to a high-speed blender, along with the fresh basil. Pulse to combine. With the blender running on low speed, slowly pour in any broth remaining in the pot after you scooped out the vegetables, followed by the cream. If you're using labneh instead of cream, add about half of the reserved pasta water and purée until smooth. Season with salt to taste.

Transfer the broccoli sauce back to the saucepan. Add the pasta. Cook over low heat for 2 minutes, stirring to coat the pasta in the sauce. Add the lemon juice and pecorino cheese. Stir to combine. The pasta should be quite saucy, so if it's looking a little dry, add another splash or two of reserved pasta water and stir to combine.

Divide the pasta among bowls. Garnish with more pecorino cheese, cracked black pepper to taste, and basil oil. Serve immediately.

Store leftovers in an airtight container in the fridge for up to 5 days.

PEPPERONI PIZZA POLENTA

SERVES 6 TO 8

I created this dish for my kids, but I love it too: using soft polenta as a base for pizza toppings eliminates the need to make or buy pizza dough, and, really, all the classic flavours of a pepperoni pizza are here. Polenta is an Italian dish made of boiled cornmeal, and its consistency can range from smooth and silky to firm enough to cut with a knife. Here we give it the Goldilocks treatment, making it neither too thin nor too thick but *just right* to spoon into, before covering it in red sauce, pepperoni, and, yes, soft melty cheese. Pair it with an easy green salad, or create a bit of contrast with a Basic Bitter Salad (page 98).

5 cups (1.25 L) hot water or broth
¼ cup (60 mL) unsalted butter or olive oil
1 teaspoon (5 mL) salt, more to taste
1¼ cups (300 mL) medium-grind cornmeal
½ cup (125 mL) grated Parmesan or pecorino cheese
¾ cup (175 mL) marinara sauce
½ cup (125 mL) sliced pepperoni
8 ounces (225 g) burrata cheese
Fresh basil, to garnish
Basil Oil (page 29), for drizzling (optional)

Preheat the oven to 500°F (260°C). In a large pot over high heat, bring the water, butter, and 1 teaspoon (5 mL) salt to a boil. Whisking continuously, slowly pour in the cornmeal. Reduce the heat to low and simmer, uncovered, stirring every 5 minutes or so to prevent lumps, until the polenta has thickened and the individual grains of cornmeal are tender, about 30 minutes. Stir in the Parmesan and add more salt to taste. The polenta will still be quite soft.

Transfer the polenta to a large cast-iron skillet. Spoon the marinara sauce over the polenta and evenly distribute the pepperoni slices overtop. Bake for 3 to 4 minutes until the sauce is bubbly and the pepperoni is cooked. Tear the burrata into four or five pieces overtop. Bake for 1 to 2 minutes more, until the cheese is melted. Remove the polenta from the oven. Top with fresh basil and drizzle with basil oil (if using). Use a large serving spoon to divide among bowls.

Store leftovers in an airtight container in the fridge for up to 5 days.

BAKE, BUBBLE, AND BRAISE

I AM ONE OF THOSE PEOPLE WHO WILL happily spend a Sunday puttering around the kitchen, cooking and baking for the sheer enjoyment of it, producing a giant weekend feast and perhaps some sweet snacks to get us through the week. That is one type of cooking. There is another type of cooking, one I do far more often, since there is only one Sunday each week and at least five other days when I am working, writing, mothering, cleaning, and so on, and I don't have the luxury of a lingering encounter with all my favourite fruits and vegetables. *This* type of cooking is all about focus and speed. I'm looking for limited steps, an efficient process, and no ingredients that require fussing over. Perhaps it's a big pot of Chicken Adobo with Black Pepper and Soy (page 168) or an extremely straightforward Roast Chicken with Pomegranate Molasses and Pistachios (page 158).

The recipes in this section are hearty and appeal to a broad range of palates, and they all deliver on flavour and can easily be paired with a pot of steamed rice or a quick salad. Many of them also result in the added bonus of leftovers, and I've included directions on how to transform the extras into something extraordinary so you can get the most out of your efforts. This chapter encourages you to make friends with your oven and use it to its full potential.

Premier
MATCHES

HOT HONEY SALMON

SERVES 6 TO 8

Who doesn't love a protein you can quickly season with a bit of spicy-sweet honey and serve after sticking it in the oven for just 12 to 14 minutes? As with all large fish dishes, it looks stunning, and it's an easy dish to pair with salads and sides. Knock together an Endive, Grapefruit, and Fennel Salad (page 106) for easy summer entertaining, or serve it with Herby Feta Orzo (page 135) or Creamy Cucumber Schmear with Everything Bagel Spice (page 48) and warm pita for something a bit heartier.

1 salmon fillet (2 to 3 pounds/ 900 g to 1.35 kg)
2 teaspoons (10 mL) salt
½ cup (125 mL) hot honey

Preheat the oven to 475°F (240°C). Line a baking sheet with parchment paper.

Place the salmon skin-side down on the prepared baking sheet. Season with the salt. Brush the fish liberally with about half of the hot honey. Bake for 12 minutes, until just cooked through. Brush with the remaining honey. Serve immediately, or let cool to room temperature and serve within 1 to 2 hours. This dish can also be stored, covered, in the fridge and served chilled the next day.

Store leftovers in an airtight container for up to 4 days.

SERVES 4 TO 6

BAKED SALMON WITH SPICY LIME VINAIGRETTE CELERY SALAD

¼ cup (60 mL) hot honey
1 tablespoon (15 mL) fish sauce
1 tablespoon (15 mL) Lovage Vinegar (page 22) or pepperoncini brine
Zest and juice of 1 lime
2 cloves garlic, finely grated
2 tablespoons (30 mL) olive oil
1 salmon fillet (1½ to 2 pounds/ 675 to 900 g)
2 stalks celery, plus any nice leaves from the centre, chopped
3 pepperoncini, thinly sliced
½ cup (125 mL) Beet Pickled Turnips (page 213)

Crunchy celery, pepperoncini, and pickles tossed in a zippy vinaigrette: this combination ticks all of the boxes and offers both contrast and cohesion when plunked on top of baked salmon. This dish has the added flexibility of being equally enjoyable when served hot, at ambient temperature, or chilled, so it's great for a crowd and looks impressive to boot. However you serve it, be sure to wait until the last minute to put the salad-y component on top so the celery leaves stay perky and the turnips don't turn everything pink. Serve alongside steamed rice or warm fluffy flatbread to soak up all the vinaigrette.

Preheat the oven to 425°F (220°C). Line a baking sheet with parchment paper.

In a small bowl, whisk together the hot honey, fish sauce, vinegar, and lime zest and juice until combined. Add the garlic. Whisk in the olive oil.

Place the salmon skin-side down on the prepared baking sheet. Drizzle about three-quarters of the vinaigrette over the fish. Bake for 15 to 18 minutes, until just cooked through.

In a medium bowl, place the celery, pepperoncini, and beet pickled turnips. Just before serving, add the remaining vinaigrette and toss to coat evenly. Transfer the salmon to a serving platter. Pile the salad on top of the salmon and serve.

Tip: This vinaigrette is so simple and can add a little zip to a lot of different dishes. Try drizzling it over roasted carrots and garnishing them with torn mint and chopped peanuts, or using it as a saucy toss for baked chicken wings or even as a dipping sauce for homemade fresh rolls stuffed full of veggies and avocado.

DILL PICKLE POACHED COD WITH SCALLION SAUCE

SERVES 4

In my opinion, pickles and fish are just a classic combination. This recipe takes only a few moments to whip up, since the cod poaches quickly in the dill pickle broth and the sauce is simple to assemble.

Dill Pickle Cod

- 2 cups (500 mL) dill pickle juice
- 2 cups (500 mL) water
- 1 cod loin (2 to 3 pounds/ 900 g to 1.35 kg)

Scallion Sauce

- 1 cup (250 mL) chopped scallions
- 1 cup (250 mL) chopped fresh cilantro leaves and stems
- 1 tablespoon (15 mL) dill pickle juice or white vinegar
- 2 cloves garlic, minced
- 4 tablespoons (60 mL) minced fresh ginger
- 1 tablespoon (15 mL) tamari or soy sauce
- 1 tablespoon (15 mL) hot honey
- ¼ cup (60 mL) olive oil
- 1 dill pickle, sliced, to serve

Line a plate with paper towels.

Make the Dill Pickle Cod: Pour the dill pickle juice into a large saucepan. Add the water (see Tip). Place the saucepan over high heat and bring the mixture to just under a boil. Add the cod. Reduce the heat to medium so the pickle juice continues to simmer but does not boil. Poach the cod in the liquid until it is opaque and just starts to flake, 3 to 4 minutes. Using a slotted spoon, transfer the cod to the prepared plate.

Make the Scallion Sauce: In a medium bowl, place the scallions, cilantro, 1 tablespoon (15 mL) of dill pickle juice, garlic, ginger, tamari, and hot honey. In a small saucepan, bring the olive oil to a boil. Carefully pour the hot oil over the scallion mixture. Stir to combine.

Arrange the cod on a medium plate. Spoon the warm sauce over the cod and scatter the pickle slices overtop. Serve immediately.

Store leftovers in an airtight container in the fridge for up to 3 days or turn them into Cod Cakes with Dilly Mayo (page 209).

Swap It: You can add all sorts of good things to the pickle poaching liquid to give it more flavour, such as 1 tablespoon (15 mL) black peppercorns, a handful of fresh dill, basil, parsley, or cilantro stems, some already-juiced lemon halves, or even onion tops that you might otherwise have discarded. Just make sure you don't put more than 1 cup (250 mL) of extra stuff in the liquid. The fish needs room to float around a bit.

SERVES 4 TO 6

ROAST CHICKEN WITH POMEGRANATE MOLASSES AND PISTACHIOS

- 1 small chicken (2 to 3 pounds/ 900 g to 1.35 kg), room temperature
- 2 tablespoons (30 mL) olive oil
- Salt and fresh cracked black pepper
- 2 tablespoons (30 mL) pomegranate molasses
- ¼ cup (60 mL) chopped pistachios, toasted (see Swap It)

In my cooking classes, people frequently mistake pomegranate molasses for balsamic reduction because it is similar in colour (dark) and viscosity (thick), but, in addition to being dramatically less expensive, pomegranate molasses is less vinegary and acidic and more fruity and tart. Because its flavour profile is not quite so overpowering, I find it easier to incorporate into a range of dishes. It's wonderful drizzled on salads like Basic Bitter Salad (page 98), dippy things like hummus or Whipped Tahini (page 18), baked or roasted fish, desserts, and of course roast chicken, where it cuts through the rich fatty flavour of the crisp skin and also adds excitement to the meat itself. Pair this recipe with a simple salad, a plate of chickpeas, or butter beans drizzled in olive oil and lemon for a low-key family dinner—perhaps with a slightly chilled bottle of gamay for the adults.

Preheat the oven to 500°F (260°C). Line a medium roasting pan with parchment paper or foil. Make a note of how many pounds your chicken is before you discard its packaging.

Rub the chicken all over with the olive oil. Liberally sprinkle it with salt and pepper, inside and out. If there is an excess of skin or fat around the cavity, trim it off and discard.

Place the chicken in the prepared pan, untrussed. Roast for 10 minutes per pound, plus an extra 8 to 10 minutes, or to an internal temperature of 165°F (74°C). Remove the chicken from the oven and let rest for about 10 minutes.

With the chicken upright and the cavity facing you, use a sharp pair of kitchen shears to begin cutting the chicken in half, lengthwise, along one side of the backbone. Flip the chicken and cut between the breast meat and the keel bone so the chicken comes apart in two more or less equal halves.

Arrange the chicken on a platter. Drizzle it with the pomegranate molasses. Sprinkle the pistachios on top. Serve immediately.

Store leftovers in an airtight container in the fridge for up to 5 days. You can also use them to make all kinds of wonderful things, like Chicken and Dumplings (page 223), Coconut Broth with Noodles, Sweet Potato, and Leftover Protein (page 216), Dill Pickle Pizza (page 189), and, of course, Chicken Broth (page 220).

Swap It: If you are short on pistachios, reach for an equivalent amount of toasted sesame seeds or chopped hazelnuts instead; they will be a fine substitute. You can also shift gears and sprinkle fresh pomegranate seeds over the chicken; they too are wonderfully crunchy, as well as juicy and tart.

ONE-POT MEATBALLS AND SPAGHETTI

SERVES 4 TO 6

This is a speedy and satisfying recipe that involves minimal effort and—even better—minimal cleanup. You can use ground beef, ground pork, or a combination of the two, depending on your taste. The meatballs are held together by grated onion, cheese, yogurt, herbs, and just enough bread crumbs to give them a bit of spring. You cook them in the sauce with the spaghetti in a very hot oven. Once the spaghetti is tender and the meatballs are cooked through, this dish gets finished with a ball of creamy burrata and a drizzle of olive oil on top.

Meatballs

1 small white onion, grated
1 slice white sandwich bread, crusts removed, torn into small pieces
¼ cup (60 mL) labneh or plain Greek yogurt
2 cloves garlic, finely grated
1 pound (450 g) medium ground pork or beef
1 cup (250 mL) grated Parmesan cheese, more to serve
Handful of chopped fresh herbs, such as flat-leaf or curly parsley or basil (optional)
1 teaspoon (5 mL) salt
Fresh cracked black pepper
Olive oil, for rolling

Pasta and Tomato Sauce

2 tablespoons (30 mL) tomato paste
1 can (28 ounces/796 mL) diced tomatoes, plus ½ can water
2 cloves garlic, finely grated
1 sprig fresh basil
Salt and fresh cracked black pepper
Parmesan rinds (optional)
Pinch of sugar (optional)
2 cups (500 mL) cherry tomatoes, halved
½ pound (225 g) spaghetti
8 ounces (225 g) burrata cheese
Extra-virgin olive oil, for drizzling

Preheat the oven to 500°F (260°C).

Make the Meatballs: In a medium bowl, combine the onion, bread, labneh, and garlic. Let the mixture thicken for about 5 minutes. Add the ground pork, Parmesan, herbs (if using), salt, and pepper to taste. Use your hands to mix it all together until just combined. Do not overmix or the meatballs will be tough. Form the mixture into 6 balls. Once they are nice and round, drizzle a little olive oil on each one and use your hands to make sure each meatball is coated in oil. This will help them keep their shape in the sauce.

Make the Pasta and Tomato Sauce: In a Dutch oven over high heat, whisk together the tomato paste, diced tomatoes, and water. Add the garlic, whole sprig of basil, salt and pepper to taste, Parmesan rinds (if using), and sugar (if using). Bring the mixture to a boil. Add the cherry tomatoes and the spaghetti and give everything a good stir. Place the meatballs on top. Transfer to the oven and cook, uncovered, for 5 minutes. Carefully remove the Dutch oven and stir the contents. Return to the oven and cook for another 5 to 8 minutes, until the pasta is tender and the meatballs are cooked through. Turn off the oven. Tear the burrata overtop of the meatballs and spaghetti. Put the dish back in the oven for 1 to 2 minutes, until the cheese gets melty.

Remove from the oven, drizzle everything with olive oil, and serve immediately with Parmesan cheese on the side.

Store leftovers in an airtight container in the fridge for up to 5 days.

SERVES 2 TO 4

BRAISED LAMB SHANKS WITH BUTTER BEANS

On this side of the Atlantic, lamb is not quite as common as beef. I've noticed in my cooking classes that many people have no idea how to prepare it and so, quite simply, they don't. This is a very good starter recipe for lamb, because it's easy enough and quite forgiving if you cook it a little less or a little more than you should. It's also a great canvas for extra flavours, like citrus or herbs or even cheese rinds or the end of a jar of olives that you might like to clear out of the fridge. The result, no matter what extras you choose to put in or leave out, is tender, flavourful lamb swimming in a rich ragout of creamy butter beans, perfect for cold-weather eating and for dipping crunchy toast into.

Lamb Shanks

2 tablespoons (30 mL) olive oil
2 to 3 lamb shanks (about 2½ pounds/1.125 kg total)
Salt and fresh cracked black pepper
¼ cup (60 mL) Red Pepper Butter (page 17) or tomato paste
4 cups (1 L) chicken broth or water
1 can (28 ounces/796 mL) diced tomatoes
2 cloves garlic, finely grated
2 cans (19 ounces/540 mL each) butter beans or cannellini beans

Optional add-ins

Cheese rinds
Fresh chopped herbs such as parsley, thyme, rosemary, or basil
Handful of pitted green or black olives
1 lemon or orange, thinly sliced, seeds removed
A few spoonfuls of roasted eggplant (see Tip on page 45)

To serve

Olive oil, for drizzling
Grated pecorino cheese, to garnish

Preheat the oven to 325°F (160°C). Line a plate with paper towels.

In a large Dutch oven over high heat, warm the oil until it starts to shimmer. Season the lamb shanks all over with salt and pepper. Use tongs to place them in the Dutch oven to brown. Reduce the heat as necessary if the oil starts to smoke. Continue browning the meat on all sides for about 4 to 5 minutes. Transfer the shanks to the prepared plate. Discard any oil in the Dutch oven and wipe out the rest with a paper towel.

Reduce the heat to medium. Add the red pepper butter to the Dutch oven. Stir in the broth, diced tomatoes, and garlic. Return the lamb to the Dutch oven. Add any optional add-ins you like and season accordingly. For instance, if you're introducing salty add-ins, like cheese rinds or olives, consider a little less salt; otherwise, a large pinch should do it. Bring the mixture to a boil and cover. Remove the Dutch oven from the stovetop and place it in the oven. Bake for 2 to 2½ hours, until the lamb is fork-tender. Add the beans. Return the lamb to the oven, uncovered, for another 20 minutes.

Ladle the lamb and its sauce into shallow bowls or wide plates with a deep rim so you can enjoy some of the lovely brothy beans. Garnish with a drizzle of olive oil and a flurry of grated pecorino cheese. Serve immediately.

Store leftovers in an airtight container in the fridge for up to 5 days. The leftover beans, in particular, are very good warmed and then spooned over crunchy olive oil–fried bread.

VINEGAR IS NOT JUST FOR SALADS

I hope that by this point in the book, you have purchased a very large, very utilitarian-looking jug of plain white vinegar. It's great for infusing (page 21), adding acidity and brightness to salads, and even as a base for a sauce, as in Store-Bought Dumplings in Homemade Chili Soy Sauce (page 195).

I've also come to really lean on white vinegar when I'm braising meat. The vinegar not only helps make tougher cuts—which are typically more flavourful—tender, it also cuts through some of the richness of a dish that has been cooked slow and low. The three recipes that follow feature a protein, a vinegar base, and a few add-ins that are straightforward to make, simple to put together, and, best of all, easy to eat!

SERVES 6

PEPPERONCINI BRAISED PORK SHOULDER

2 pounds (900 g) pork shoulder, bone removed and reserved, cut into 3-inch (8 cm) cubes (see Tip)
2 teaspoons (10 mL) salt, more for the braise
Fresh cracked black pepper
1 tablespoon (15 mL) ground cumin
1 tablespoon (15 mL) sweet paprika
2 tablespoons (30 mL) olive oil
1 cup (250 mL) water
¾ cup (175 mL) white vinegar
2 tablespoons (30 mL) sugar or pure liquid honey
1 small yellow onion, quartered
4 cloves garlic, smashed
1 jar (17 ounces/500 mL) pepperoncini, plus the brine
2 guajillo chilies (optional)

To serve

½ bunch fresh cilantro, stems minced and leaves roughly chopped
Juice of 1 lime
½ small yellow onion, thinly sliced

Pork shoulder is a great cut of meat because it's inexpensive, has lots of marbling and therefore flavour, and can easily feed a crowd. You don't need a huge portion to feel satisfied, and that is especially true when it's swimming in a rich, brothy, vinegary sauce laced with spicy pepperoncini. As with all good braises, there's really not much active work here—you can let it bubble away without having to babysit it too much. Serve this dish next to some roasted sweet potatoes or fried plantains to sop up all that good braising liquid, or pair it with the like-minded flavours found in dishes like Crunchy Brussels Sprout and Raw Corn Salad (page 94).

Line a large plate with paper towels.

In a medium bowl, toss the cubed pork with 2 teaspoons (10 mL) of the salt, a few cracks of black pepper, the cumin, and the paprika.

Warm the olive oil in a large Dutch oven over high heat until it starts to shimmer. Carefully add the pork in batches, spacing the cubes out so it browns and does not steam. Reduce the heat to medium-high (lower as needed if the oil starts smoking), and cook the pork for 3 to 5 minutes, turning it so that it is more or less evenly browned on all sides. Use tongs to transfer the seared pork to the prepared plate. Once the pork is browned, turn off the heat, discard any oil in the Dutch oven, and wipe out the rest with a paper towel.

Return the pork and the reserved bone to the Dutch oven and place it over high heat. Add the water, vinegar, sugar, onion, garlic, pepperoncini and brine, guajillo chilies (if using), and a big pinch of salt. Bring the mixture to the gentlest of boils, give it a stir, then reduce the heat to low to maintain a simmer. Cook, covered, for 2 to 2½ hours, lifting the lid every once in a while to give everything a poke and a stir, until the meat is fork-tender. Remove and discard the bone.

Serve hot, garnished with a sprinkling of cilantro, a drizzle of lime juice, and a few slices of crunchy onion.

Store leftovers in an airtight container or the Dutch oven in the fridge for up to 5 days. If you're looking to invigorate your leftovers after a day or two, try repurposing them by making Pepperoncini Pork Tacos (page 228).

Tip: To make this even lower-effort, you can skip cubing the pork and just heavily season and then sear the pork shoulder in its entirety. You'll need to add about 1 to 1½ extra hours to the braise time.

SERVES 4 TO 6

CHICKEN ADOBO WITH BLACK PEPPER AND SOY

- ¾ cup (175 mL) white vinegar or Chive Blossom Vinegar (page 22)
- ¾ cup (175 mL) dark soy sauce
- 1 head of garlic, peeled, cloves separated and thinly sliced
- 1 green chili, thinly sliced
- 8 skin-on, bone-in chicken thighs, skin removed and reserved for Crispy Garlic Rice with Chicken Skin Crunch (page 227)
- 2 tablespoons (30 mL) olive oil
- 1 cup (250 mL) water
- 5 bay leaves
- 1 teaspoon (5 mL) whole black peppercorns
- 2 tablespoons (30 mL) sugar or pure liquid honey
- Fresh cracked black pepper

Adobo, a dish indigenous to the Philippines, comes in a myriad of versions. Some recipes include ingredients like coconut milk, turmeric, or pineapple that shape its flavour profile, but this is more or less the first version I tasted and I love its simplicity. As far as I know, all versions of the recipe rely on some kind of protein, some kind of vinegar, and soy sauce or salt. When I tried homemade adobo in New York for the first time I expected it to be astringent, but the white vinegar mellows with cooking, tempers the saltiness of the soy, tenderizes the chicken, and also helps extract flavour from all the other ingredients to form a luscious sauce perfect for spooning over Crispy Garlic Rice with Chicken Skin Crunch (page 227).

In a medium bowl, whisk together the vinegar, soy sauce, garlic, and chili. Add the chicken and toss to coat. Let marinate at room temperature for at least 20 minutes and up to 1 hour.

Line a plate with paper towels.

In a large Dutch oven over high heat, warm the oil until it starts to shimmer. Remove the chicken from the marinade and pat it dry with paper towels. Reserve the marinade. Sear the chicken for 1 to 2 minutes on each side, until lightly browned, reducing the heat to medium-high if the oil starts to smoke. Transfer the chicken to the prepared plate. Discard any oil in the Dutch oven and wipe out the rest with a paper towel.

Add the reserved marinade to the Dutch oven and bring it to a boil over high heat. Reduce the heat and let it simmer for about 5 minutes. Add the water, bay leaves, peppercorns, sugar, and seared chicken. Continue simmering, uncovered, for 20 to 25 minutes, until the chicken is tender and cooked through. Add cracked black pepper to taste. Serve hot over Crispy Garlic Rice with Chicken Skin Crunch (page 227).

Store leftovers in an airtight container or Dutch oven in the fridge for up to 5 days.

BRAISED BEEF WITH VINEGAR AND PEPPERS

SERVES 4 TO 6

Like all busy people, I find it useful to have recipes that only require you to do a simple task or two in a big pot, add some ingredients, and then put the pot somewhere it can simmer away gently for a few hours until someone needs to eat. This is a very good version of this type of recipe, in which beef stews softly and vegetables sweeten and become tender in a vinegary broth.

2 pounds (900 g) chuck roast
1 tablespoon (15 mL) salt
Fresh cracked black pepper
1 tablespoon (15 mL) sweet paprika
2 tablespoons (30 mL) olive oil
4 cups (1 L) beef broth or water
1 medium yellow onion, cut into 6 wedges
2 red bell peppers, cut into quarters
2 green bell peppers, cut into quarters
4 cloves garlic, thinly sliced
¾ cup (175 mL) white vinegar
2 tablespoons (30 mL) sugar or pure liquid honey

Rub the beef all over with the salt, lots of cracked black pepper, and the paprika. Place the beef on a plate and let it rest at room temperature for at least 1 hour, but no more than 2.

Line a plate with paper towels.

Warm the olive oil in a large Dutch oven over high heat. Once the oil starts to shimmer, gently place the beef in the Dutch oven to brown. Reduce the heat as necessary if the oil starts to smoke, and continue browning the meat for 5 to 7 minutes, turning every so often to ensure each side gets browned. Use tongs to lift the roast out of the Dutch oven and transfer it to the prepared plate. Discard any oil in the Dutch oven and wipe out the rest with a paper towel.

Return the beef to the Dutch oven. Add the beef broth, onion, red and green bell peppers, garlic, vinegar, and sugar. Bring the mixture to a boil over high heat, cover, and reduce to a simmer. Let simmer, covered, for 2½ to 3 hours, or until the beef is fork-tender. Serve hot.

Store leftovers in an airtight container in the fridge for up to 5 days. Future you will be most grateful if you use leftovers to make Braised Beef Nachos (page 231).

MAKE IT TASTE LIKE TAKEOUT

I'VE LIVED IN SOME OF THE GREATEST CITIES in the world, where you can walk a block in any direction and trip over takeout options for all kinds of wonderful foods. Now I live in a quiet little town, and while it's great in a different way than, say, New York City or Berlin—and we do have unexpectedly good sushi across the street and an exceptional shawarma spot—takeout culture isn't really a thing. Delivery options are limited, expensive, and often take upwards of an hour to arrive, which not only defeats the purpose but also makes everything that was once crispy soggy, and everything that was once hot tepid at best. Pressure makes diamonds, however, and the absence of Uber Eats in my life has had the surprising upside of forcing me to create really straightforward, really craveable recipes that rival anything I could scroll and select, and at a fraction of the price.

This chapter is all about creating restaurant-worthy meals at home, without the wait or the expense. There's also the added benefit of knowing exactly what's going into your food to make it so delicious. Takeout tastes really good for a reason: it often contains a lot of oil and a lot of sugar. I'm not saying those things aren't included in this chapter, but you do get to choose the quality of your oils and your sugars, as well as the rest of your ingredients, and you'll find your dollar stretches a lot further when you aren't paying someone to make and deliver your food.

Finally, for all my fellow Type A folks out there, another perk of making your favourite restaurant-style dishes at home is that you can adjust the flavours to suit your preferences. Most restaurants are cooking to appeal to as wide a demographic as possible and they are not considering you, the individual, and what you might like best. But you! You can make yourself a top priority! Add more chilies, reduce the salt, leave out the cilantro, add extra cilantro, cook the steak rare, double the cheese, whatever you like. Swing for the fences! You are the chef!

Some of these recipes, like Spicy Crunch Noodles (page 196) and Store-Bought Dumplings in Homemade Chili Soy Sauce (page 195), are very fast to pull together and can be assembled from things you may well already have. If you put these dishes out in combination with some crunchy chopped cucumber or quickly steamed greens doused in a little chili crisp and sesame oil, and offer up a couple of cold, cheap beers and a few packets of chopsticks from your last Chinese takeout, you will have one of my ideal meals in less than ten minutes.

Some require a bit more time, but are well worth it. See what all the hype is about with Dill Pickle Pizza (page 189) or make good on that promise you made to yourself to eat more vegetables with Sub Salad with Mortadella and Black Olives (page 177). Whatever you choose to make, have a bit of fun with it and relax. I find I am most likely to be ordering takeout after a stressful or hectic day, but if I take a breath and reframe cooking as something enjoyable, the way I would view a crossword or some other little puzzle to be solved, then the entire experience, from cooking to eating, becomes one of relaxation and pleasure.

SUB SALAD WITH MORTADELLA AND BLACK OLIVES

SERVES 4 TO 6

I'm often inspired to make dishes in a roundabout way. A "sub salad" is what line cooks often call a salad that someone orders in lieu of the usual side served with the main protein of a dish. One day when I was working alongside my talented friend Chef Zach Smith, he called out "Halibut . . . sub salad!" and I only registered the sub salad portion of the call. I started thinking about how great it would be to make a salad that tasted like a submarine sandwich. You know, with black olives, cubes of soft, shiny cheese, red onions, and a sub sauce–adjacent red wine vinaigrette? Maybe with a huge pile of thinly sliced mortadella on top? So that's pretty much exactly what this next recipe is.

Sub Sauce Vinaigrette

½ cup (125 mL) extra-virgin olive oil
¼ cup (60 mL) red wine vinegar
1 tablespoon (15 mL) Basil Oil (page 29)
2 teaspoons (10 mL) dried oregano
Salt and fresh cracked black pepper

Sub Salad

1 head of iceberg lettuce, thinly sliced
7 ounces (200 g) mozzarella or provolone cheese, cubed
½ cup (125 mL) pitted black olives, sliced
½ cup (125 mL) pepperoncini, sliced, plus 1 tablespoon (15 mL) brine
½ small red onion, thinly sliced
Handful of fresh basil, thinly sliced, more basil leaves to garnish
8 ounces (225 g) mortadella, very thinly sliced

Make the Sub Sauce Vinaigrette: In a small bowl, whisk together the olive oil, red wine vinegar, basil oil, oregano, and salt and pepper to taste.

Make the Sub Salad: Place the lettuce, mozzarella, olives, pepperoncini and brine, onion, and basil in a large bowl. Pour the dressing over the salad. Toss until everything is evenly coated. Transfer the salad to a large plate. Pile the mortadella on top and garnish with fresh basil leaves. Serve immediately.

SERVES 4 TO 6

SEVEN LAYER DIP

- ½ (16-ounce/454 g) can refried beans
- 2 tablespoons (30 mL) water
- 1 cup (250 mL) labneh
- ½ cup (125 mL) salsa
- 1 avocado, pitted, peeled, and chopped
- ½ cup (125 mL) halved cherry tomatoes
- ½ cup (125 mL) pitted black olives, sliced
- 4 scallions, sliced
- 1 cup (250 mL) shredded iceberg lettuce
- Handful of fresh cilantro, chopped
- Juice of 1 lime (optional)
- Hot Vinegar (page 22) or hot sauce, for drizzling
- Corn chips or warm tortillas, to serve

Inspired by my husband Oscar's passion for grocery store seven layer dip, but with a few upgrades like labneh instead of sour cream, real avocado, fresh cilantro, and homemade Hot Vinegar (page 22), this dish is one of those nostalgic hits that everyone can get behind. Serve it at a party, chips 'n' dip style, or pair it with warm tortillas, a Steak Night Steak (page 203), or Crunchy Brussels Sprout and Raw Corn Salad (page 94) for a quick weeknight dinner that everyone will love.

In a small bowl, mix together the refried beans and water. The beans should be loose enough to dollop.

Spread out the labneh on a large platter. Spoon the beans and salsa overtop so that they are more or less evenly distributed. Scatter the avocado, tomatoes, olives, scallions, lettuce, and cilantro on top. Drizzle everything with lime juice (if using) and hot vinegar. Serve immediately with corn chips or warm tortillas.

Tip: Freeze leftover refried beans for your next batch of Seven Layer Dip. You can also spread a thin layer on a tortilla and fold it over with a melty cheese like mozzarella or Monterey Jack, then fry it gently for a quick bean and cheese quesadilla.

SPEED ADJ.

Tip: You will inevitably have leftover phyllo from this recipe—head over to page 261 to use it up in an easy, incredible Phyllo Cake.

PHYLLO WRAPPED FETA WITH HOT HONEY

SERVES 4

If this book offers you one thing you can carry forward into the rest of your culinary adventures, I hope it is that spectacular food does not have to be particularly complex. I love streamlined recipes like this one because they are manageable to put together—in a fit of hunger or in a hurry—and you can taste each of the components. Here, soft, salty feta gets wrapped in crispy, buttery phyllo pastry before it's topped with roasty, toasty sesame seeds for extra pleasure and crunch, and then drizzled with just a little sweet and spicy honey and spiked with lemon. Although wrapping the feta in phyllo takes a moment or two, it's no more challenging than wrapping a birthday gift. Pair this dish with a handful of greens tossed in Spicy Vinaigrette (page 26) and a sharp squeeze of lemon for an ideal meal.

½ cup (125 mL) melted unsalted butter
Pinch of salt
8 sheets phyllo pastry
5½ ounces (150 g) feta, cut into 4 blocks
3 tablespoons (45 mL) sesame seeds
¼ cup (60 mL) hot honey
2 teaspoons (10 mL) lemon juice

Preheat the oven to 375°F (190°C). Line a baking sheet with parchment paper.

Place the melted butter in a small bowl. Whisk in the salt.

On a clean work surface, lay a sheet of phyllo in front of you so that its length runs along the edge of your work surface. Brush the pastry very lightly with the melted butter. Lay another sheet of phyllo on top and fold it in half as though you are closing a book. Brush the phyllo with butter again—it should be shiny with the butter but not dripping. Place a block of feta about 4 inches (10 cm) from the bottom edge of the phyllo. Fold the sides of the phyllo over the feta snugly, brushing it again with a little butter to help the phyllo stick to itself. Fold the bottom flap of phyllo over the feta so it seals in the bottom, again brushing with a little butter to help it stick. Finally, take the remaining flap of phyllo at the top of the feta and wrap it around the feta so you have a nice little square-ish package. Don't worry if it's not perfect; after you bake it, it will look golden brown and flaky and wonderful even if it is a little shaggy. Brush the phyllo all over with butter and sprinkle sesame seeds on top. Place the phyllo wrapped feta on the prepared baking sheet. Repeat to assemble 3 more portions.

Bake for 20 minutes, until the phyllo is crispy and the cheese has softened (see Tip).

In a small bowl, whisk together the hot honey and lemon juice. Drizzle over the phyllo wrapped feta and serve immediately.

If you're not going to eat all of the phyllo wrapped feta as it comes out of the oven, store the unbaked feta packages in an airtight container in the fridge for a few days or tightly wrap and freeze them until you plan to serve them. Simply let the refrigerated or frozen pastry come to room temperature on the counter and bake according to the recipe.

LABNEH AND SCALLION STUFFED FLATBREADS WITH SPICY OIL

MAKES 4 FLATBREADS

Years ago, I was couch surfing in Luxembourg during the winter and stumbled upon a tiny Nepalese restaurant. I had just enough euros for a bowl of soup and some cheese-stuffed naan. Both were delicious, but the stuffed naan really stuck with me. I'd had things stuffed in bread before—I grew up with Hot Pockets and Pizza Pops and, of course, Twinkies—but something about the shape of the naan, the hit of cumin, the tangy cheese, the soft stretchy dough, and the setting all combined to make the dish last in my memory.

This recipe has evolved over the years, most notably with a switch from cottage cheese to labneh since you're more likely to find that in my fridge, and, yes, sometimes I use store-bought pizza dough instead of making my own. When I'm cooking at home, I find the recipes that you allow to stray a little from their inspiration are the ones that stand the test of time, because they grow with you to satisfy the needs you have right now.

Flatbread Dough

1 cup (250 mL) lukewarm water
1 tablespoon (15 mL) pure liquid honey or sugar
1 tablespoon (15 mL) active dry yeast
2 cups (500 mL) all-purpose flour, divided, more for dusting
3 tablespoons (30 mL) olive oil, divided, more for preparation
1 teaspoon (5 mL) salt

Labneh and Scallion Filling

¾ cup (175 mL) chopped scallions or ramps or grated yellow onion
½ cup (125 mL) labneh or plain Greek yogurt
2 medium cloves garlic, finely grated
Pinch of ground cumin
Pinch of ground red chilies
Pinch of salt

Spicy Oil

¾ cup (175 mL) chopped scallions or ramps
¼ cup (60 mL) sesame seeds, toasted
2 teaspoons (10 mL) Aleppo pepper
1 tablespoon (15 mL) Everyday Vinegar (page 21)
Pinch of sugar (optional)
Pinch of salt
½ cup (125 mL) olive oil

Make the Flatbread Dough: Place the water in a medium bowl. Add the honey and yeast and whisk until the yeast dissolves. Add 1 cup (250 mL) of the flour. Whisk for about 3 minutes, until you have a thick paste. This will help the dough start to build gluten and prevent you having to knead as much. Loosely cover the bowl with a clean cloth or kitchen towel and set aside for 1 hour to rise.

After 1 hour, uncover the dough. Add 2 tablespoons (30 mL) of the olive oil and the salt. Whisk to combine. Add the remaining 1 cup (250 mL) flour. Using a spatula or a wooden spoon, stir until the mass forms a sticky dough.

Sprinkle a little flour on a clean work surface like a countertop or a large cutting board. Tip the dough out onto the surface. Using floured hands, knead the dough for about 3 minutes, adding just enough flour to keep it from sticking to the work surface or your hands.

Shape the dough into a large ball, drizzle it with a little olive oil, and rub the olive oil all over the surface of the dough to keep it from drying out. Place the dough back in the bowl, cover again with a cloth, and let rise for another 20 to 30 minutes while you make the filling.

Recipe continues

Make the Labneh and Scallion Filling: In a medium bowl, place the scallions, labneh, garlic, cumin, red chilies, and salt. Stir to combine.

Assemble the flatbreads: Divide the dough into 4 equally sized balls. Drizzle each ball with a little olive oil so they don't dry out while you fill them. To fill the dough, sprinkle a little flour on your work surface. Place a dough ball on top. Sprinkle the dough with a little more flour. Use a rolling pin to roll out the dough into a circle that is 6 inches (15 cm) in diameter. Place ¼ of the filling in the middle of the circle. Dip your pointer finger in a bit of tap water and then run it around the edge of the circle—this will help seal the filling in. Pull the edges of the dough circle up and over the filling so that all the dough edges meet, then pinch the dough with your fingers to make sure they seal together. Set aside and repeat with the 3 remaining dough balls.

When you are ready to cook the flatbreads, warm 1 tablespoon (15 mL) of olive oil in a large cast-iron skillet over high heat until it starts to shimmer. Working one at a time, use a rolling pin to roll out one of the filled dough balls into a large oval shape about ¾ inch (2 cm) thick. Gently place it in the hot skillet. Reduce the heat to medium. Fry for 2 to 3 minutes until the bottom is golden brown. Flip and fry for another 2 to 3 minutes, until the other side is golden. Transfer the cooked flatbread to a clean plate. Repeat with the 3 remaining dough balls.

Make the Spicy Oil: In a small bowl, mix the scallions, sesame seeds, Aleppo pepper, Everyday Vinegar, sugar (if using), and salt.

Place the oil in a small saucepan over high heat and bring to a boil.

Carefully pour the oil over the ingredients in the bowl. Stir briefly and let stand for a moment or two to let the flavours infuse.

To serve: Put out your flatbreads alongside the spicy oil while they are still warm.

Leftovers lose a little something once they hit the fridge, but the breads can be rewarmed in an ungreased cast-iron skillet for 1 to 2 minutes on each side. The oil is just as if not more flavourful the next day since it's had longer for the flavours to commingle.

Tip: This technique of stuffing flatbread is basically a Pandora's box of deliciousness. Don't be shy about using this recipe as a springboard to stuff other culinary delights into a flatbread. Options might include a few spoonfuls of leftover Pepperoncini Potato Salad with Feta and Cilantro (page 124) that have been mashed with a fork, ricotta with a hot honey drizzle, and, of course, marinara, melty cheese, and pepperoni—for your own custom Pizza Pop–inspired creation.

LAHMACUN

SERVES 4 TO 6

The first time I ate lahmacun, a Middle Eastern flatbread topped with ground spiced meat, I was in the Turkish market near my apartment in Berlin. Small women stood behind huge smoking griddles, deftly tossing flatbreads over the heat to achieve the perfect crust and then piling them in giant, delicious stacks to keep warm. Before serving them, the women would roll up the lahmacun, perhaps after drizzling some lemon or a little sauce inside. Then they would wrap them in foil and hand them over in exchange for a couple of euros.

The flavour of rich lamb spiked with peppers and allspice was familiar from my own childhood, but the combination of all those tastes in a street food snack was a revelation. This version, which stays fairly true to my memory of the original, comes together quickly thanks to the use of a blender. It has become a family favourite in our house as an alternative to pizza night. My daughters roll their own dough and spread the lamb, and I handle the cast-iron cookery while my husband brings it all together with a sauce (see Tip).

Flatbread Dough

- 1 cup (250 mL) lukewarm water
- 1 tablespoon (15 mL) pure liquid honey or sugar
- 1 tablespoon (15 mL) active dry yeast
- 2 cups (500 mL) all-purpose flour, divided, more for dusting
- 2 tablespoons (30 mL) olive oil, more for drizzling
- 1 teaspoon (5 mL) salt

Spiced Lamb Topping

- 3 red bell peppers, seeds removed and roughly chopped or 3 roasted red peppers
- ½ small white onion, roughly chopped
- 2 cloves garlic
- Handful of fresh flat-leaf parsley, chopped, more to garnish
- 2 tablespoons (30 mL) olive oil, more for cooking the lahmacun
- ¼ cup (60 mL) Red Pepper Butter (page 17) or tomato paste
- ½ pound (225 g) ground lamb
- 1 teaspoon (5 mL) ground allspice
- 1 teaspoon (5 mL) cinnamon
- 1 teaspoon (5 mL) Aleppo pepper
- 1 teaspoon (5 mL) ground cumin
- 1 teaspoon (5 mL) salt
- ½ teaspoon (2 mL) ground red chilies
- 1 teaspoon (5 mL) sweet paprika
- Juice of 1 lemon, for drizzling

Make the Flatbread Dough: Place the water in a medium bowl. Add the honey and yeast and whisk until the yeast dissolves. Add 1 cup (250 mL) of the flour. Whisk for about 3 minutes, until it turns into a thick paste. This will help the dough start to build gluten and keep you from having to knead as much. Loosely cover the bowl with a clean cloth or kitchen towel. Let rise for 1 hour.

After 1 hour, uncover the dough. Add 2 tablespoons (30 mL) of the olive oil and the salt. Whisk to combine. Add the remaining 1 cup (250 mL) flour. Using a spatula or a wooden spoon, stir until the flour is incorporated and a sticky dough forms.

Sprinkle a little flour on a clean work surface, like a countertop or a cutting board, and tip out the dough. Using floured hands, knead for about 3 minutes, adding just enough flour to keep it from sticking to the work surface or your hands. Form it into a big ball, drizzle it with a little olive oil, and rub the olive oil all over the surface of the dough to keep it from drying out. Place the dough back in the bowl, cover with a cloth, and let rise for an additional 20 to 30 minutes while you make the topping.

Make the Spiced Lamb Topping: Place the peppers, onion, garlic, parsley, and olive oil in a high-speed blender or food processor and pulse briefly so it looks a bit like a chunky paste. Add the red pepper butter, lamb, allspice, cinnamon, Aleppo pepper, cumin, salt, chilies, and paprika. Purée until just combined.

Recipe continues

Divide the dough into 8 to 10 balls. Drizzle each ball with a little more olive oil and set aside. Place a large cast-iron skillet over medium-high heat.

Working with one ball at a time, use a rolling pin to roll the dough into a rough oval shape about ¼ inch (5 mm) thick. Spread a thin layer of the topping on the dough. Drizzle just enough olive oil into the cast-iron skillet to coat the surface of the pan and conduct the heat, but not so much that you wind up frying the lahmacun. Gently transfer the dough to the hot skillet, ensuring the toppings remain face-up. Cook until the bottom is nicely browned and the top is cooked, about 3 to 5 minutes. You may need to adjust the heat up or down a little depending on your stove. Once you find your stove's ideal temperature for lahmacun, stick with it while you repeat the process of rolling and cooking the remaining dough balls one at a time.

Drizzle each piece of warm lahmacun with lemon juice and top with a few parsley leaves. Cut the flatbread into wedges or roll it up and serve warm.

Leftovers can be wrapped tightly and stored in the fridge for up to 5 days. To reheat, simply cook the lahmacun in a hot, unoiled cast-iron skillet over high heat for 1 to 2 minutes.

Tip: My husband, Oscar, loves Big Macs and frequently tries to "Mac" things by adding homemade Mac sauce and thinly sliced iceberg lettuce. While not traditional, we've found "Mac"-ing lahmachun to be really delicious. To make Oscar's version of Mac sauce, mix together about ½ cup (125 mL) mayonnaise, 1 tablespoon (15 mL) yellow mustard, 1 tablespoon (15 mL) ketchup or tomato paste, 1 tablespoon (15 mL) dill pickle juice, and 1 chopped-up pickle. Spoon about 2 tablespoons (30 mL) (or more!) of this sauce on your warm lahmacun and top it with a handful of thinly sliced iceberg lettuce and, if you like, a few thinly sliced yellow onions that have been shocked in ice water to take out the sting. Sprinkle with sesame seeds if you have them, then roll it all up and enjoy.

ABANDONED GROVE
2022RESERVE

DILL PICKLE PIZZA

SERVES 4 TO 5

When I first heard about dill pickle pizza, you could put me firmly in the "curious skeptic" category. But when Andrew Thorne, one of my favourite chefs, made me try his version, I was an easy convert. The combination of melty cheese, creamy dill pickle white sauce, acidic pickles, herby dill, crunchy iceberg lettuce, and, of course, a satisfying carb-y crust is beyond delicious and has become a family favourite that I hope you will enjoy too!

Pizza Dough (see Tip)

- 1 cup (250 mL) lukewarm water
- 1 tablespoon (15 mL) pure liquid honey or sugar
- 1 tablespoon (15 mL) active dry yeast
- 2 cups (500 mL) all-purpose flour, divided, more for dusting
- 2 tablespoons (30 mL) olive oil, more for drizzling
- 1 teaspoon (5 mL) salt

Toppings

- 1 cup (250 mL) shredded rotisserie chicken or leftover Roast Chicken with Pomegranate Molasses and Pistachios, skin removed (page 158)
- ½ small yellow onion, thinly sliced
- 1 jar (1 L) dill pickles, thinly sliced, pickle juice reserved
- 2 cups (500 mL) shredded mozzarella cheese

Dill Pickle White Sauce

- 2 tablespoons (30 mL) unsalted butter
- 2 tablespoons (30 mL) all-purpose flour
- 1 cup (250 mL) whole (3.25%) milk, warmed
- Pinch of salt

To serve

- Handful of fresh dill, chopped
- 1 cup (250 mL) shredded iceberg lettuce
- Hot honey, for drizzling

Make the Pizza Dough: Place the water in a medium bowl. Whisk in the honey and yeast until the yeast dissolves. Add 1 cup (250 mL) of the flour. Whisk for about 3 minutes, until it turns into a thick paste. This will help the dough start to build gluten and keep you from having to knead as much. Loosely cover the bowl with a clean cloth or kitchen towel. Let rise at room temperature for 1 hour.

After 1 hour, uncover the dough. Add 2 tablespoons (30 mL) of the olive oil and the salt. Whisk to combine. Add the remaining 1 cup (250 mL) flour. Using a spatula or a wooden spoon, stir until the flour is incorporated and a sticky dough forms.

Sprinkle a little flour on a clean work surface, like a countertop or a cutting board, and tip out the dough. Using floured hands, knead for about 3 minutes, adding just enough flour to keep it from sticking to the work surface or your hands. Form it into a big ball, drizzle it with a little olive oil, and rub the olive oil all over the surface of the dough to keep it from drying out. Place the dough back in the bowl, cover with a cloth, and let rise for an additional 20 to 30 minutes while you make the topping.

Prepare the Pizza Toppings: Place the chicken and the onions in a small bowl. Add just enough dill pickle juice to cover them. Set aside to marinate.

Make the Dill Pickle White Sauce: In a small saucepan, melt the butter over medium heat. Whisk in the flour. Continue whisking for 2 to 3 minutes, until the mixture looks dry. Whisking continuously, slowly pour in the milk. Continue whisking for 5 minutes, until the sauce has thickened. Give the chicken and onions in the reserved pickle juice a final stir, then use a fine-mesh strainer to strain the marinating liquid into the sauce. Set the chicken and onions aside for the pizza topping. Continue cooking and whisking for 2 to 3 minutes until the sauce has reduced by a quarter. Add a pinch of salt and whisk to combine.

Assemble the Pizza: Preheat the oven to 425°F (220°C).

Recipe continues

Roll out the dough to a diameter of about 14 inches (35 cm) and place it on a pizza tray. Spoon the sauce over the dough and spread it in an even layer. Evenly distribute the chicken and onion mix overtop. Sprinkle the shredded cheese over everything. Scatter the sliced pickles over the cheese.

Bake for 12 to 15 minutes, until the cheese is bubbling and the crust is golden brown. Remove from the oven and let stand a minute or two. Scatter the fresh dill and iceberg lettuce overtop. Drizzle with the hot honey. Serve immediately.

Store leftovers in the fridge in an airtight container for up to 5 days.

Tip: Feel free to buy the pizza dough or use a ready-made crust. You can also buy a good-quality jar of alfredo sauce instead of making your own white sauce—simply put 1 cup (250 mL) of alfredo sauce in a small saucepan and bring to a boil. Add the marinating liquid and cook long enough to reduce by about a quarter, then use as directed to sauce the pizza.

Swap It: Skip the chicken and onions and put the pickles, cheese, and white sauce on your Any Vegetable Galette dough (page 90) for a flaky, elegant Dill Pickle Galette!

CRISPY PORK SALAD WITH PICKLES, HERBS, AND SPICY MAYO

SERVES 4 TO 6

I am always trying to make my husband, Oscar, food he loves, but I also want to make him food that has lots of vegetables. This salad is more or less a Vietnamese bahn mi—a combo of pickles, heaps of herbs, savoury pâté, spicy mayo, and meat or tofu on a crispy baguette—which tops Oscar's list of favourite foods.

Try not to be put off by all the different components here. They come together fairly quickly—even the pork takes only a few minutes to bread and then another 6 to 8 minutes to fry gently (but do refer to the Tip below if preparing the meat feels overwhelming at this exact moment). You can make the pickles ahead of time or simply use whatever pickles you have on hand.

Pickled Carrots and Turnips

1 medium carrot, peeled and thinly sliced
1 medium white turnip, peeled and julienned
½ cup (125 mL) white vinegar
½ cup (125 mL) sugar

Spicy Mayo

½ cup (125 mL) mayonnaise
1 tablespoon (15 mL) sriracha sauce or other hot sauce
Zest of 1 lime

Hoisin Dressing

½ cup (125 mL) hoisin sauce
Juice of 1 lime
4 tablespoons (60 mL) reserved carrot and turnip pickling liquid, divided (from above)

Crispy Pork

8 ounces (225 g) pork loin cutlets
¼ cup (60 mL) all-purpose flour
2 eggs
1 tablespoon (15 mL) hoisin sauce
¾ cup (175 mL) panko or homemade bread crumbs
2 pinches salt, more to taste
Olive oil, for frying

Make the Pickled Carrots and Turnips: Place the carrots and turnips in a small heat-proof bowl.

In a small saucepan over high heat, bring the vinegar and sugar to a boil. Immediately pour the mixture over the vegetables. Let cool to room temperature, or until you're ready to serve, making sure to reserve the pickling liquid for the hoisin dressing. (The pickles can be made ahead of time. Once they have cooled to room temperature, store them in their pickling liquid in an airtight container in the fridge until ready to use, up to 3 months.)

Make the Spicy Mayo: In a small bowl, whisk together the mayonnaise, sriracha sauce, and lime zest to combine.

Make the Hoisin Dressing: In a small bowl, whisk together the hoisin sauce, lime juice, and 2 tablespoons of the reserved carrot and turnip pickling liquid to combine.

Make the Crispy Pork: Lay the pork cutlets on a clean cutting board. Hold a rolling pin with a firm grip and give each pork cutlet a few whacks until they are roughly ¾ inch (2 cm) thick.

Set out 3 medium bowls; place the flour in the first, the eggs and hoisin sauce in the second, and the panko in the third. Add a pinch of salt to both the flour and the panko. Use a fork to beat the egg mixture, and to stir the others to ensure the salt is evenly distributed.

Recipe continues

Salad

½ medium head of iceberg lettuce, chopped
⅓ English cucumber, thinly sliced
3 scallions, thinly sliced
Handful of fresh mint
Handful of fresh cilantro
Handful of fresh basil

To serve (optional)

Toasted baguette
Pork pâté

Working quickly, dip the pork in the flour. Give it a shake to remove any excess. Next, dip it in the egg mixture. Shake to remove any excess. Finally, dip the pork in the panko, using your hands to press the panko into the egg and make sure each cutlet is fully coated. Place the breaded cutlet on a clean plate. Line a second plate with paper towels.

In a heavy-bottomed skillet over medium-high heat, heat the olive oil until it starts to shimmer. Fry the pork for 2 to 3 minutes per side, until crispy and golden. Transfer it to the prepared plate. Sprinkle with salt and let rest.

Assemble the Salad: Use a big spoon to schmear about half of the spicy mayo on a large platter. Place the lettuce, cucumber, and scallions in a pile on top. Spoon the pickled carrots and turnips and 2 tablespoons (30 mL) of the pickling liquid over everything. Briefly tear the fresh herbs and scatter them overtop of the dish.

Thinly slice the pork. Add it to the salad. Use the big spoon to drizzle the remaining spicy mayo and the hoisin dressing over everything. Serve as is, or with a baguette and pork pâté.

Tip: If breading and frying pork cutlets seems like too much, you can tear up about half of a leftover roast chicken and toss it in about 2 tablespoons (30 mL) each of lime juice, Spicy Vinaigrette (page 26), and hot honey, then use in place of the pork in this recipe. Alternatively, cut a block of medium tofu into about 8 slices and cook it in a large skillet over high heat with about 2 tablespoons (30 mL) each of lime juice, Spicy Vinaigrette, and hot honey. Allow the liquid to come to a boil and then reduce heat to a simmer for 2 to 3 minutes, until the tofu has warmed through.

STORE-BOUGHT DUMPLINGS IN HOMEMADE CHILI SOY SAUCE

SERVES 4 AS AN APPETIZER

This recipe is very much inspired by the time I spent in New York City as a culinary student. When I moved there, one of the first things I did was set up a "dumpling crawl" with a friend wherein we would eat at all the best dumpling spots in Lower Manhattan. Clutching a MapQuest printout with our target locations circled and starred, we went from shop to shop eating hot dumplings swimming in tangy, spicy, and savoury sauce. To this day, I love a dumpling. This recipe offers a quick way to get all those good dumpling feelings, without too much fuss or a trip to New York, in about ten minutes. You can use any kind of Chinese dumpling: while my preference is pork and scallion, I encourage you to pick your favourite and jump off from there. Make this dish with a pot of white rice and quickly sautéed cabbage or greens for an easy but incredible dinner.

2 tablespoons (30 mL) white or black vinegar
2 teaspoons (10 mL) ground red chilies
Pinch of sugar
2 tablespoons (30 mL) tamari or soy sauce
¼ cup (60 mL) olive oil
1 cup (250 mL) water
1 bag (20 ounces/567 g) dumplings, flavour of your choice
Sesame seeds, to serve

Place a large saucepan of salted water over high heat and bring to a boil. In a large cast-iron skillet over high heat, whisk together the vinegar, chilies, and sugar. Bring the mixture to a boil so that the sugar dissolves. Add the tamari, olive oil, and water. Stir to combine. Reduce the heat to medium and let simmer while you make the dumplings.

Once the salted water in the saucepan is at a rolling boil, add the dumplings and cook according to the package instructions, minus 2 minutes, stirring occasionally so that they don't stick to the bottom of the saucepan. Use a slotted spoon to transfer the dumplings to the skillet with the sauce. Continue simmering the dumplings in the sauce for 2 minutes.

Transfer the dumplings and sauce to a serving plate or bowl. Sprinkle with sesame seeds. Serve warm.

Store leftovers in an airtight container in the fridge for up to 5 days.

SERVES 2

SPICY CRUNCH NOODLES

¼ cup (60 mL) tahini (see Tip)
2 tablespoons (30 mL) chili crisp
2 tablespoons (30 mL) hot honey
2 cloves garlic, finely grated
1 tablespoon (15 mL) tamari
1 tablespoon (15 mL) white vinegar
2 packages (3 ounces/85 g each) instant ramen noodles, seasoning packets discarded

To serve
Sesame seeds
Chopped scallions

Dinner in five minutes? Yes you can! This recipe for crunchy, creamy, spicy noodles worthy of your favourite downtown takeout joint takes almost no time to prepare and uses pantry staples you probably already have. Put a pot of water on while you read this recipe, and you'll have a meal ready before you can turn the page.

Bring a medium saucepan of salted water to a boil.

While you're waiting for the water to boil, make the sauce. In a medium bowl, whisk together the tahini, chili crisp, hot honey, garlic, tamari, and vinegar.

Cook the noodles according to the package instructions. Drain the noodles, reserving about ½ cup (125 mL) of the noodle water.

Add about ¼ cup (60 mL) of the reserved noodle water to the sauce. Whisk to form a creamy sauce. Transfer the noodles to the sauce. Toss until they are fully coated. If you want the noodles to be a bit saucier, add the remaining noodle water and toss again. Divide the noodles among bowls. Garnish with the sesame seeds and chopped scallions. Serve immediately.

Store leftovers in an airtight container in the fridge for up to 5 days.

Tip: If you don't have tahini, peanut butter or even cashew butter are great alternatives. They will still add creaminess to your sauce, plus a bit of rich, nutty flavour too.

VOLUME
FM AM
88 92 96 100 104 108 MHz
55 65 80 100 130 160 KHz

RICE CAKES WITH CRISPY PORK AND SOY

SERVES 6

Korean rice cakes, known as garaetteok, are a cylinder-shaped cake made of puréed white rice, traditionally simmered in a spicy sauce and served as a street food. I first ate them at Chef David Chang's restaurant Momofuku, and I fell in love with their very satisfying and compulsively eatable chew right away. Pairing them with a rich, slippery, and spicy gravy that is studded with seasoned ground pork and smothering them in chili crisp is not traditional by any means, but it has become one of the things that people most frequently ask me to make for them. This suits me well, since this recipe takes about 15 minutes from start to finish and, while I like to make people happy, I also like to do it quickly.

3 cups (750 mL) chicken broth or water
2 teaspoons (10 mL) cornstarch
2 tablespoons (30 mL) olive oil
1 pound (450 g) ground pork
Salt
Pinch of ground red chilies
2 tablespoons (30 mL) tamari or soy sauce
1 tablespoon (15 mL) oyster sauce
2 tablespoons (30 mL) Chive Blossom Vinegar (page 22) or white vinegar
Pinch of sugar (optional)
1 bag (21 ounces/600 g) frozen cylindrical Korean rice cakes
1 bunch scallions, chopped
½ cup (125 mL) chili crisp, more to serve
Crispy onions, to serve

In a measuring cup, whisk together the chicken broth and cornstarch. Set aside.

In a large skillet over high heat, warm the oil just until it shimmers. Add the pork. Season well with salt and the red chilies. Cook the pork, without stirring, for 2 to 3 minutes so that it sears. Use a wooden spoon or perforated spatula to break up the pork. Add the tamari, oyster sauce, vinegar, and sugar (if using) to the meat. Stir. Cook for 1 minute. Add the broth mixture. Stir to combine. Bring the broth to a boil.

Rinse the frozen rice cakes thoroughly so that they separate—they do not have to be fully thawed, but you don't want them in a big frozen lump when you introduce them to the sauce. Add the rice cakes to the skillet. Continue cooking for 5 to 7 minutes over high heat, until the rice cakes have heated through and the sauce has thickened, stirring occasionally so that the rice cakes do not stick. Stir in the scallions and chili crisp. Remove from the heat. Serve immediately with more chili crisp on the side, if desired. Garnish with crispy onions.

Store leftovers in an airtight container in the refrigerator for up to 5 days. Be sure to reheat the leftovers before serving: the rice cakes become very tough at cooler temperatures.

SERVES 4

STEAK TARTARE WITH SESAME AND PICKLES

½ pound (225 g) lean beef, such as tenderloin or top sirloin
½ small white onion, thinly sliced
1 tablespoon (15 mL) extra-virgin olive oil
½ teaspoon (2 mL) salt
Fresh cracked black pepper
1 cup (250 mL) shredded iceberg lettuce
2 egg yolks
1 medium dill pickle, sliced into rounds, plus a splash of pickle juice
1 tablespoon (15 mL) sesame seeds, toasted

To serve

Spicy dill pickle chips (I prefer Miss Vickie's) or plain kettle chips
Yellow mustard

I will order steak tartare—a dish traditionally made of chopped raw steak, capers, shallots, Dijon mustard, and raw egg yolk—any time I see it on a menu. It's one of those dishes that seems complex and fancy, but is actually pretty straightforward, especially since you don't need to cook anything.

My version deviates from the classic rendition but still honours its flavours, and pulls in more than a few nods to another restaurant dish I love—the McDonald's Big Mac—in the form of crisp dill pickles, raw white onion, iceberg lettuce, and, of course, toasted sesame seeds. When you load it onto a spicy dill pickle chip and add a smidge of yellow mustard, it is absolute heaven for the tartare lovers among us.

Remove the beef from its packaging and place it on a clean plate in the freezer for 10 to 20 minutes to help it become a bit firmer and easier to cut. Place the onion in a small bowl of ice water and let soak for at least 5 minutes.

Place the chilled beef on a cutting board (see Tip). Use a sharp knife to remove all sinew and extra fat. Dice the steak into ¼-inch (5 mm) pieces. Transfer the meat to a small bowl. Add the olive oil, salt, pepper to taste, and a splash of pickle juice. Toss to coat evenly.

Spread the shredded lettuce onto about two-thirds of a serving platter and arrange the beef in a mound on top. Make 2 wells in the meat. Gently place an egg yolk in each well. Scatter the pickles, drained onion, and sesame seeds evenly over the meat. Fill the remaining empty space on the platter with chips of your choice and set out a dish or two of yellow mustard. Serve immediately.

Tip: When you take the beef out of the freezer, replace it with the platter you intend to serve it on. An icy cold platter is by no means required, but it's a simple and elegant touch that takes no real time or effort to achieve. If you'd rather skip the raw egg yolks, finely grate some Cured Egg Yolks (page 77) overtop of the dish to bring in a little flavour and fat.

STEAK NIGHT STEAK

SERVES 2

When I feel like a proper steak, I go all in on a good grass-fed ribeye with lots of marbling, and then I don't do too much to it except cook it well and baste the heck out of it with butter and vinegar. Topped with a little Spicy Vinaigrette (page 26) and paper-thin slices of peppery radish, this is a steak recipe that is perfectly bold in its simplicity.

1 ribeye steak (1½ pounds/675 g)
Salt and fresh cracked black pepper
2 tablespoons (30 mL) olive oil
2 tablespoons (30 mL) butter
2 tablespoons (30 mL) Chive Blossom Vinegar (page 22) or white vinegar
¼ cup (60 mL) Spicy Vinaigrette (page 26)
4 radishes, thinly sliced

Season the steak liberally with salt and let sit at room temperature for 1 to 2 hours. Use a paper towel to blot the steak and remove any excess moisture.

Heat the olive oil in a large cast-iron skillet over high heat until it just shimmers. Season the steak again with salt and lots of pepper. Gently lay the steak in the skillet. Cook, without moving the steak, for 2 to 3 minutes, until you see the edges start to brown. Reduce the heat to medium and continue cooking for another 2 to 3 minutes, until the steak is evenly caramelized. Flip the steak, increase the heat to high, and cook the second side in the same manner as the first. Turn off the heat and tip out any extra oil into a heatproof bowl or jar to discard later. Quickly add the butter and vinegar to the skillet. Use a large spoon to baste the steak with the buttery juices for about 2 minutes. Transfer the steak to a wire rack and let rest for 5 to 10 minutes.

Thinly slice the steak against the grain and transfer it to a serving plate. Spoon the spicy vinaigrette over the steak and sprinkle the radishes on top. Serve warm.

Store leftovers in an airtight container in the fridge for up to 5 days.

Tip: Use leftovers to make Chilled Steak with Eggplant Dip, Arugula, and Pistachios (page 232).

USE IT TWICE TO USE IT ALL

LEFTOVERS, PARTICULARLY AMONG HOME COOKS, seem to be a polarizing topic. People have *strong feelings* about eating cold, chewy slabs of lasagna from the fridge, or perhaps tearing the remaining meat off a roast chicken and tucking it neatly alongside some crisp bacon, frilly lettuce, and juicy tomato on some heavily mayonnaised soft brown bread. For me, the feelings are overwhelmingly favourable. After a day or two in the fridge, the flavours of a dish often deepen and textures inevitably soften. And, of course, you can't beat the convenience of food that has already been prepared.

This is a chapter that teaches you to reimagine the potential of leftovers as a new beginning. The key to my strategy for invigorating leftovers is to repurpose them as ingredients that you can build an entirely new and different dish around. This approach is used in top kitchens around the world—those of grandmothers and restaurants alike—because it is economical and also helps avoid the scourge of what I call "leftover fatigue." No one with any sense of imagination or passion for novelty wants to eat the same thing over and over again, and, let's be honest, some things are impossible to simply reheat without sacrificing their intention and integrity. Trying to recook Dill Pickle Poached Cod with Scallion Sauce (page 157) the next day will result in dry fish at best, and at worst something that manages to both be rubbery and completely fall apart at the same time. But! The same cod, folded into fluffy grated potato, mixed with a bit of mayonnaise and salt, and then breaded and fried until crisp—as in Cod Cakes with Dilly Mayo (page 209)—results in a dish that is comforting, compelling, and convenient in equal measure.

Most of the recipes in this chapter will reference an earlier recipe in the book and show you how to add a bit of this and a bit of that to transform it into an entirely new meal. Turn Braised Beef with Vinegar and Peppers (page 171) into a crowd-pleasing pan of crunchy, cheesy, and slightly spicy Braised Beef Nachos (page 231), or resuscitate just about any forgotten protein by making Coconut Broth with Noodles, Sweet Potato, and Leftover Protein (page 216). If perhaps you haven't yet made the original recipe, don't worry: you can either sub in something else or simply start with the original. In most cases it won't add too much time or effort to get the result you crave. This section also encourages you to use up things you might have hanging about in your kitchen—revive a cold, congealed pot of white rice by making Crispy Garlic Rice with Chicken Skin Crunch, or create some freezer real estate by emptying your zip-top bag of vegetable scraps into a nourishing pot of Chicken Broth (page 220).

The recipes that follow are meant to tantalize, but also to educate. Once you make a handful of them, you'll find it easier to make a meal out of leftovers. You will also find yourself feeling more creative and tenacious in your cooking, with a fridgeful of great starting points for amazing meals.

Swap It: This recipe welcomes seafood substitutions and even additions, if you wish. Try using leftover salmon, trout, or haddock—anything flaky will work. You can also chop up an equal amount of denser seafood, like scallops, lobster, or shrimp.

I keep my cod cakes very plain because cod and potatoes are among my favourite foods and I don't like to add much to them, but if you are craving a bit more zip, add a handful of chopped chives, a few chopped-up pickles, half a diced onion that you've fried softly in butter until it has lost its crunch, or even a dash or two of your favourite hot sauce.

COD CAKES WITH DILLY MAYO

SERVES 2 TO 4

Fish cakes are the best possible use for leftover cod. Not only do they come together in next to no time, requiring no great skill, but they are crisp on the outside, tender on the inside, and universally popular. Try them on their own with a handful of dressed greens, next to some freshly boiled green peas, or stuff them into fluffy sub buns with lots of pickles, Mac sauce (page 186), and shredded iceberg lettuce.

Cod Cakes

1 cup (250 mL) Dill Pickle Poached Cod with Scallion Sauce (page 157, see Tip)
1 cup (250 mL) boiled and grated russet potato, or leftover mashed potato
1 tablespoon (15 mL) mayonnaise
1 teaspoon (5 mL) salt, more to taste
Fresh cracked black pepper

Dilly Mayo

1 cup (250 mL) mayonnaise
1 tablespoon (15 mL) pickle juice
2 teaspoons (10 mL) Basil Oil (page 29)
Handful of chopped fresh dill

Breading

3 to 4 egg whites
1 cup (250 mL) all-purpose flour
1 cup (250 mL) panko or homemade bread crumbs
1 pinch of salt, more for finishing
½ cup (125 mL) olive oil

Make the Cod Cakes: In a medium bowl, place about half of the cod, the grated potato, and the mayonnaise, and season with 1 teaspoon (5 mL) of salt and pepper to taste. Use a large spoon or your hands to mix well so that the cod can easily be moulded. Gently fold in the remaining cod. Check the seasonings and add salt almost to the point of over-seasoning—both the cod and the potato will benefit from this treatment. Form the mixture into small round cakes, about 2 inches (5 cm) in diameter and ¾ inch (2 cm) thick. Place them on a clean plate and chill them in the fridge while you make the dilly mayo.

Make the Dilly Mayo: In a small bowl, stir together the mayonnaise, pickle juice, basil oil, and dill.

Bread the Cod Cakes: Remove the cod cakes from the fridge. Place the egg whites, flour, and panko in separate medium bowls. Add a large pinch of salt to the flour. Working with one or two cakes at a time, and using two forks to move the cakes around, dip the cakes first in the flour. Shake off any excess. Next, dip them in the egg whites. Shake off any excess. Finally, dip them into the panko. Use your hands to re-form the cod cakes a bit. They will inevitably have lost a bit of their shape in the breading process, and compressing them will help the top layer of crumbs stick, ensuring a crisp coating.

Line a plate with paper towels.

In a large skillet over high heat, warm the oil until it starts to shimmer. Reduce the heat to just above medium. Wait about 30 seconds, then fry the cod cakes 4 or 5 at a time, adjusting the heat as necessary, until they are golden brown on both sides, about 1 to 2 minutes per side. Transfer the cod cakes to the prepared plate. Sprinkle with salt. Repeat with the remaining cakes.

Serve immediately with dilly mayo on the side and your preferred side dish.

SERVES 4

SALMON WITH CUCUMBERS, PICKLED BEETS, AND YOGURT

¼ small yellow onion, thinly sliced
Pinch of sugar
¼ cup (60 mL) brine from Beet Pickled Turnips (page 213) or white vinegar
½ English cucumber
Pinch of salt
1 cup (250 mL) plain Greek yogurt
1 pound (450 g) or so Hot Honey Salmon (page 153), chilled
1 cup (250 mL) Pickled Beets (page 213)
Zest and juice of 1 lime
Handful of fresh dill or celery leaves, roughly chopped
Extra-virgin olive oil, for drizzling
Fresh cracked black pepper

These flavours—salmon, tart dairy, pickled beets, cucumber, onion, and dill—are vaguely Eastern European, which means they are right in my wheelhouse. Nothing is complicated here, but plattering all of this good stuff and using bright pickled beets and their juice adds some wow factor. Serve this dish for lunch or dinner as is, or make it part of a brunch spread alongside some toasted Montreal-style bagels.

Place a large platter in the freezer to chill.

Place the sliced onion in a small bowl of ice water for about 5 minutes to take away the sting. Drain. Place the onions back in the bowl and sprinkle them with the sugar. Toss gently to coat. Pour the pickle brine or vinegar overtop and set aside.

Lay the cucumber out horizontally on a sturdy surface like a cutting board. Give it a few firm whacks with a heavy object, like a rolling pin. Use your hands to tear it into bite-sized pieces. Transfer the cucumber to a bowl and sprinkle it with the salt. Set aside.

Spread the yogurt on the chilled platter. Using your hands, gently flake the salmon into slightly larger than bite-sized pieces and sprinkle them on top. Evenly distribute the pickled beets around the platter. Drain any juice from the cucumbers and add them around the plate as well. Add the lime zest and juice. Drain the pickling liquid from the onions and scatter them on top. Sprinkle the dill over everything. Drizzle the platter with olive oil and top with a few cracks of black pepper. Serve immediately.

Tip: A liberal dusting of everything bagel spice is a great addition to this dish.

OIL
VINEGAR

PICKLED BEETS

MAKES 4 CUPS (1 L)

- 6 to 8 medium yellow or candy cane beets
- 1½ cups (375 mL) vinegar, divided
- Pinch of salt
- ½ cup (125 mL) sugar

There are all sorts of places you can buy pickled purple beets, which is good because I find making any volume of them to be a bit messy, so I avoid it. I much prefer to invest my time and effort into pickling golden and candy cane beets, since they are so pretty and don't stain your hands or your cutting board with nearly the same intensity. Try them anywhere you would use a regular pickled beet, but especially in Salmon with Cucumbers, Pickled Beets, and Yogurt (page 210).

Place the whole beets and ½ cup (125 mL) of the vinegar in a medium saucepan. Add enough cold water to cover, as well as a hearty pinch of salt. Bring to a boil over high heat, then reduce to just above a simmer for about 30 minutes, until the beets can be easily pierced with a paring knife. Strain off the liquid. You can either run the beets under water to cool them immediately or let them hang out in a colander in your sink until cool enough to handle.

When the beets are cool, use a paring knife to remove the skin and cut the beets into bite-sized wedges. Place the beets in a 4-cup (1 L) jar with a tight-fitting lid.

In the same saucepan over high heat, bring the remaining 1 cup (250 mL) vinegar and the sugar to a boil. Pour over the beets and let cool to room temperature. Screw on the lid and store in the refrigerator until ready to use or up to 1 month. Be sure to dip in and out of the jar with a clean spoon.

BEET PICKLED TURNIPS

MAKES 4 CUPS (1 L)

- 1 small purple beet, sliced into thick matchsticks
- 2 medium turnips, sliced into thick matchsticks
- 1 cup (250 mL) white vinegar
- 1 cup (250 mL) sugar

These are so simple to make and brighten any dish with both their fuchsia colour and their hit of acidity. If you've never tried a turnip pickle before, they are so good: crunchy and peppery and all the things you need a pickle to be. The colour won't take immediately, so if you want them to be super pink, make them the night before you plan to use them.

Place the beets and turnips into a 4-cup (1 L) jar with a tight-fitting lid.

In a small saucepan over high heat, bring the vinegar and sugar to a boil. Carefully pour the boiling liquid over the vegetables. Let stand on the counter, uncovered, for about 1 hour. Screw on the lid and store in the refrigerator until ready to use or up to 1 month. Be sure to dip in and out of the jar with a clean spoon.

SALMON SALAD WITH ASPARAGUS AND NEW POTATOES

SERVES 4

This salad is centred on leftover salmon, but the flavours make it feel like something you might be served on a bistro patio in France. Simple vegetables, green olives, crisp lettuce, and a splash of vinegary Dijon mustard enter the picture as supporting actors, and a flurry of Cured Egg Yolks (page 77) adds richness and excitement. Pair this with a good baguette and a cold glass of Sancerre for a simple meal worth savouring.

1 pound (450 grams) new potatoes
Handful of asparagus
1 tablespoon (15 mL) Chive Blossom Vinegar (page 22) or white vinegar
2 tablespoons (30 mL) Dijon mustard
Handful of lettuce, such as baby gem or Boston bibb
1 pound (450 grams) or so Hot Honey Salmon (page 153), chilled and flaked into large chunks
Handful of green olives, such as Castelvetrano, pitted
Salt and fresh cracked black pepper
Extra-virgin olive oil, for drizzling
Cured Egg Yolks (page 77), to garnish

Place a large platter in the freezer to chill.

Place the potatoes in a large saucepan of salted water. Bring the water to a boil. Reduce the heat to a simmer. Cook for 10 to 12 minutes, until the potatoes are tender all the way through, but not soggy. Use a large slotted spoon to transfer the potatoes to a colander to drain. Bring the saucepan of water back up to a rolling boil.

Meanwhile, prepare an ice bath by filling a medium bowl about halfway with ice and adding enough tap water to cover the ice. Snap the bottoms off the asparagus—they will naturally break where the woodiness begins—and then trim the bottoms if you would like them to look neat. Drop the asparagus in the boiling water. Blanch for 2 to 3 minutes, until it is bright green and crisp-tender. Use tongs to remove the asparagus from the saucepan. Immediately plunge it into the ice water, until fully chilled.

In a small bowl, whisk together the chive blossom vinegar and Dijon mustard.

Spread out the lettuce leaves on the chilled platter. Tear or cut the potatoes in half. Place the potatoes, asparagus, salmon, and olives on top of the lettuce. Season everything well with salt and pepper to taste. Spoon the Dijon mixture overtop, followed by a generous drizzle of olive oil. Finely grate about ¼ of a cured egg yolk overtop. Serve either immediately or shortly after dressing the salad. This dish will hold well at room temperature if you are having a casual meal.

Swap It: This salad is a great place for extra Olive Vinaigrette (page 55) to land: use about ¼ cup (60 mL) in lieu of both the Dijon mustard and vinegar mixture and the olive-oil drizzle.

SERVES 4 TO 6

COCONUT BROTH WITH NOODLES, SWEET POTATO, AND LEFTOVER PROTEIN

Soups and broths are a great way to stretch leftover proteins and also to dress them up a bit, so to speak. This basic coconut curry soup can be made in about fifteen minutes, and it has the sorts of flavours that combine well with just about any protein, be it chicken, pork, steak, fish, or tofu. You can also omit the protein entirely and simply add a thinly sliced zucchini to the hot broth when it's finished cooking. I've kept this soup very mild to appeal to a wide range of spice tolerances, but it's loaded with flavour from the fish sauce and the punch of lime. Piling all sorts of inviting textures on top, like jalapeños, Beet Pickled Turnips (page 213), cilantro, and thinly sliced cabbage, takes this simple soup to the next level, leaving you with a dish that feels vibrant and satisfying.

2 cups (500 mL) leftover cooked protein, such as chicken, cod, pork, steak, or soft tofu
3 tablespoons (45 mL) coconut oil or olive oil
3-inch (8 cm) piece of fresh ginger, sliced
1 medium sweet potato, peeled and cut into 2-inch (5 cm) cubes
Pinch of salt
1 tablespoon (15 mL) yellow curry powder
1 teaspoon (5 mL) turmeric
4 cups (1 L) Chicken Broth (page 220) or water
2 cans (13.5 ounces/400 mL each) full-fat coconut milk
1 tablespoon (15 mL) pure liquid honey or sugar
4 ounces (115 grams) rice vermicelli or rice stick noodles (see Tip)
2 tablespoons (30 mL) fish sauce
1 tablespoon (15 mL) Hot Vinegar (page 22) or pepperoncini juice
Zest and juice of 2 Limes

To serve

Handful of fresh cilantro
½ cup (125 mL) Beet Pickled Turnips (page 213)
½ cup (125 mL) thinly sliced green cabbage
2 scallions, thinly sliced
1 jalapeño pepper, thinly sliced
Chili crisp
Lime wedges

Chop or tear your protein into bite-sized pieces.

In a large saucepan over high heat, warm the coconut oil. Add the ginger. Fry for 3 to 5 minutes until golden brown, stirring so that it does not burn. Use a slotted spoon to remove the ginger and discard.

Add the sweet potato and a big pinch of salt to the ginger-infused oil. Cook for 3 to 5 minutes, until they just start to soften. Add the curry powder and turmeric. Stir. Let the spices toast for about 30 seconds, then add the chicken broth, coconut milk, and honey. Bring the soup to a boil. Reduce heat to a simmer and cook for 10 to 12 minutes, until the sweet potato is al dente, but not soft.

Rinse the noodles well with water. Add them to the saucepan, along with your protein. Stir so that the noodles separate. Continue cooking for about 2 minutes, or until the noodles are tender and the protein is warmed through. Add the fish sauce, hot vinegar, and lime zest and juice. Give everything a good stir.

Divide the soup among bowls. Top each serving with fresh cilantro, beet pickled turnips, some green cabbage, scallions, and jalapeño. Serve with chili crisp and lime wedges. Leftovers can be stored in an airtight container in the fridge for up to 5 days.

Swap It: If you don't have noodles, simply omit them from the soup and ladle the broth over fluffy steamed white or brown rice instead.

JUST BUY THE WHOLE CHICKEN

You can purchase chicken packaged in all sorts of different ways, and I am certainly not above grabbing the occasional family-size pack of chicken legs or thighs if they are on sale. However, in general, the best way to experience a chicken is to buy the whole chicken. Even if you decide to watch a video tutorial on how to break the chicken down into its constituent parts, you still get the benefit of being able to use the whole thing, which, in my opinion, is a good deal more interesting and cost-effective than that vacuum pack of boneless skinless chicken breasts.

- Save raw chicken skin in a small airtight container and keep it in your freezer until you decide to make Crispy Garlic Rice with Chicken Skin Crunch (page 227). You can also render it down and roast potatoes in it, or toss it with wilted greens, or even use it instead of butter when you make the dumplings portion of Chicken and Dumplings (page 223).
- Use raw or roasted bones, including the wings, alongside the contents of that zip-top bag of vegetable and herb stems you've been accumulating in your freezer to make rich, golden Chicken Broth (page 220).
- Add thinly sliced raw chicken breasts to stir-fries or soups during the last few minutes of cook time to add some quick protein.
- Heavily season raw, skin-on chicken thighs and fry them in a cast-iron skillet on both sides until cooked through. Serve them alongside some sharp Dijon mustard, a couple of olives, and a vinegary green salad with a few sprigs of tarragon for an ideal meal.
- Leftover cooked meat can be stripped from the bones and used in a myriad of ways (for example, in the following few recipes), but it can also form the foundation of many non-recipe recipes like chicken salad sandwiches, be served over rice with a dollop of Honey Harissa (page 25) and a drizzle of Whipped Tahini (page 18), or be stuffed into lettuce wraps with leftover Spicy Mayo (page 191), thinly sliced cucumber, and whatever pickled things you have around.

MAKES ABOUT 8 CUPS (2 L)

- 1 medium roast chicken carcass
- 1 medium yellow onion, skin on, halved
- 2 carrots, cut into 3-inch (8 cm) lengths
- 3 stalks of celery, cut into 3-inch (8 cm) lengths
- 2 tablespoons (30 mL) Everyday Vinegar (page 21) or white vinegar
- 10 cups (2.5 L) cold water or store-bought low-sodium chicken broth
- 1 chicken, vegetable, or mushroom bouillon cube (optional)

CHICKEN BROTH

I always have a jar or two of homemade broth in my fridge. It is, of course, a great jump-start to a meal, since it has endless uses. You can use it as a soup or stew base, as a liquid for cooking pasta or beans in, and even for steaming vegetables or fish. But it is also a meal on its own—rich, sippable, cozy, and deeply restorative. It's a great gift for new parents too. My recipe for chicken broth is very loose because it's meant to rely on ingredients you have on hand. If your chicken carcass is a bit bigger or smaller, or you don't have the vegetables that I suggest using on hand, it will be of no great detriment to the broth. You can get quite a bit of flavour out of chicken bones, and I find adding a splash of vinegar both helps to enhance that flavour and keeps everything in balance. Otherwise, I like to keep my broth neutral, so as not to limit its many uses. You can of course add a great deal more flavour by adding other ingredients to this basic recipe (see Swap It).

Place the chicken carcass, onion, carrots, celery, vinegar, water, and bouillon cube (if using) in a large stockpot or a Dutch oven. Bring it to a boil over high heat. Reduce the heat to a simmer. Let simmer, uncovered, for about 1 hour. Use a fine mesh strainer to remove the solids and discard them.

Let the broth cool to room temperature. Store it in an airtight container in the fridge until ready to use, up to 1 week.

Swap It: The broth pot is a wonderful alternative to the compost bucket for herbs and vegetables (and even, dear reader, I must confess, the occasional Tupperware of leftovers!). The only vegetables I suggest you avoid adding are starchy ones like squash, potatoes, or zucchini, since they will slowly disintegrate in your broth and make it cloudy. Here is a non-exhaustive list of other ingredients to add to your broth, should you be inclined:

- Fresh herbs or herb stems, especially parsley, thyme, and sage
- A splash of tamari or soy sauce
- A red or green chili
- Lemons or lemon peels
- Firm vegetables like rutabaga, turnips, and parsnips
- Leafy greens like kale, bok choy, and Swiss chard
- Other alliums like leeks, garlic, and scallions

CORNING

Tip: Streamline this recipe by serving simply Chicken Broth (page 220) and dumplings, or skip the onions, carrots, and peas and just add extra celery.

CHICKEN AND DUMPLINGS

SERVES 4 TO 6

This recipe is comfort at its best—hot, brothy soup laced with vegetables and chunks of chicken, studded with big fluffy dumplings. A smattering of fresh dill adds brightness and interest, even in the darkest depths of winter. I like to make this dish the day after I roast a chicken. Although store-bought broth or a bouillon cube will always be fine, there is a richness that comes out when you make chicken and dumplings from scratch. With all its good smells and bits of vegetables bobbing in the broth, the simple becomes sublime.

Soup

2 tablespoons (30 mL) olive oil or schmaltz (page 139)
3 stalks celery, diced
2 carrots, diced
1 small yellow onion, diced
2 pinches salt
6 cups (1.5 L) Chicken Broth (page 220)
2 cups (500 mL) leftover chicken, torn into bite-sized pieces
1 cup (250 mL) frozen peas

Dumplings

2 cups (500 mL) all-purpose flour
1 tablespoon (15 mL) baking powder
1 teaspoon (5 mL) baking soda
1 teaspoon (5 mL) salt
Pinch of sugar
1 cup + 2 tablespoons (280 mL) whole (3.25%) milk
2 tablespoons (30 mL) melted butter, bacon fat, or schmaltz (page 139)

To serve

Handful of chopped fresh dill
Fresh cracked black pepper

Make the Soup: In a large Dutch oven over high heat, warm the olive oil until it starts to shimmer. Add the celery, carrots, and onion. Season with a large pinch of salt. Cook for 3 to 5 minutes, stirring continuously to ensure the vegetables do not brown but just start to soften. Add the chicken broth. Prepare the dumplings while you're waiting for the broth to come to a boil.

Prepare the Dumplings: In a medium bowl, whisk together the flour, baking powder, baking soda, salt, and sugar. In a small bowl, whisk together the milk and melted butter. Pour the wet ingredients into the dry ingredients. Use a spatula to stir until just combined.

Add the leftover chicken, peas, and another pinch of salt to the boiling broth. Stir to combine. Reduce the heat to a simmer. Use a large spoon to drop about 6 or 7 large spoonfuls of the dumpling mixture into the broth. Cover and let simmer for about 15 minutes, until the dumplings are puffed and cooked through.

To serve: Divide the chicken and dumplings among bowls. Garnish with the dill and lots of cracked black pepper. Serve immediately.

Leftovers can be stored in the Dutch oven or an airtight container in the fridge for up to 5 days.

Swap It: If you haven't got whole milk, dumplings are relatively forgiving. You can swap in an equal amount of buttermilk, or you can use roughly a 3:1 ratio of labneh, sour cream, or yogurt and water. There will be no discernible taste difference and you'll still end up with a nice, fluffy dumpling.

SERVES 4

SOFT TOFU AND NOODLES IN BROTH

- 8 cups (2 L) Chicken Broth (page 220)
- 2 tablespoons (30 mL) tamari or soy sauce
- Salt
- 2 packages (3 ounces/85 g each) instant ramen noodles, seasoning packets discarded
- 1 cup (250 mL) thinly sliced green cabbage
- 1 package (16 ounces/450 g) soft tofu, cut or broken into 4 large chunks
- Chili crisp, to serve

Brothy soups are a universal favourite in my house. Not only do they feel nourishing, but they are economical to make and quick to pull together. This soup, born of a 6:00 p.m. "what's for dinner tonight?" dilemma, leverages quick-cooking ramen noodles, a handful of thinly sliced cabbage, and soft tofu, and comes together in about the same amount of time it takes to set the table and rummage around in the fridge for your favourite jar of chili crisp or hot sauce. The broth here is obviously the star, but I love that the soft tofu brings a bit of creaminess and acts as a counterpoint to the slurpy noodles and just-cooked cabbage.

In a large saucepan, bring the broth to a boil. Add the tamari. Season with salt to taste. Add the noodles and cook according to the package instructions, minus 1 minute. Give the noodles a good stir. Add the cabbage. Stir again. Gently add the tofu. Cook for 1 minute. Serve immediately alongside some chili crisp or your favourite spicy condiment.

CRISPY GARLIC RICE WITH CHICKEN SKIN CRUNCH

SERVES 2 TO 4

Chicken skin is arguably one of the best parts of the chicken—it's full of flavour and texture, and is just downright enjoyable to eat—but not all recipes create an environment that benefits this humble yet extraordinary ingredient. So if you happen to be boiling, braising, or putting chicken skin anywhere it might run the risk of becoming wet and flabby, please remove it and store it in an airtight container in your fridge for a few days, or your freezer for up to a month, until you have the chance to fry it all up and make this delicious rice.

½ cup (125 mL) or so chicken skin
1 tablespoon (15 mL) olive oil
Pinch of salt, more for sprinkling
2 cloves garlic, thinly sliced
1 green chili, thinly sliced
2 scallions, thinly sliced
2 cups (500 mL) cooked long-grain rice

Place a fine-mesh sieve over a small bowl. Using a sharp knife, roughly chop the chicken skin into 1-inch (2 cm) pieces.

In a large skillet over medium heat, gently cook the chicken skin in the olive oil, covered, for about 10 minutes. Stir. Increase the heat to medium-high and continue cooking and stirring until the chicken skin is crisp and golden brown. Carefully pour the crisp skin and the fat through the sieve and reserve the strained chicken fat. Sprinkle the chicken skin with salt. Transfer the cooked chicken skin to a clean plate while you make the rice.

Wipe out the skillet with a paper towel. Add 3 tablespoons (45 mL) of the strained chicken fat to the skillet and place it over high heat. Once the fat starts to shimmer, reduce the heat to medium. Add the garlic and chili. Fry gently until the garlic turns golden and starts to smell fragrant, 1 to 2 minutes. Add the scallions and a pinch of salt. Fry for 1 minute. Use a slotted spoon to transfer the garlic, chili, and scallions to the plate with the chicken skins.

Add the rice to the hot skillet. The rice should sizzle when it hits the skillet, but the pan shouldn't be so hot that it starts to burn. You may need to adjust the heat up or down a little, depending on your stove. Use a spatula to press the rice into the pan so that it starts to form a crust. Cook for about 5 minutes, without stirring, until the crust is golden brown. Gently flip the rice. Don't worry if the rice breaks up when you flip it. Cook on the other side for another 4 to 5 minutes, until golden. Use a spoon to break up any large pieces of rice. Stir in the chicken skins, garlic, chili, and scallions. Stir and serve hot with Chicken Adobo with Black Pepper and Soy (page 168) or simply with a fried egg and a bottle of your favourite hot sauce on the side.

SERVES 4

PEPPERONCINI PORK TACOS

2 cups (500 mL) or so leftover Pepperoncini Braised Pork Shoulder (page 166), plus 2 cups (500 mL) braising liquid
White vinegar (optional)
Salt (optional)
1 to 2 tablespoons (15 to 30 mL) olive oil
8 to 10 corn tortillas
1 cup (250 mL) crumbled queso fresco, grated paneer, or shredded Monterey Jack cheese

To serve

1 bunch fresh cilantro, roots trimmed and roughly chopped
Juice of 1 lime
½ small white onion, thinly sliced
1 jalapeño pepper, thinly sliced
1 avocado, pitted, peeled, and thinly sliced

There are more than a few recipes in the world—and, yes, in this book—that are actually better the second time around. Pepperoncini Braised Pork Shoulder (page 166) is perfectly delicious spooned over fluffy white rice or served next to some roasted sweet potatoes and corn tortillas, but when you give it a day or two to really let the flavours meld and then purée all those peppers and juices into a dipping sauce for cheesy-porky tacos stuffed with raw onions, hot peppers, creamy avocado, and fistfuls of cilantro, it is out of this world. I like to make these tacos on a casual night, when I don't mind standing at the stove flipping and loading tortillas that usually get eaten just about as fast as I can cook them. Serve with extra napkins and cold beer.

Remove the pork from the braising liquid and place it in a small bowl. Use a fork to shred the pork. Set aside.

Place the braising liquid along with any remaining solids in a high-speed blender. Purée until smooth.

Transfer the liquid to a medium saucepan over high heat and bring to a boil. Reduce heat to a simmer and cook for 5 minutes to allow it to thicken and the flavours to commingle. Taste the braising liquid. It should be delicious, but add a little white vinegar, water, or even salt to taste (if using). Spoon enough of the puréed braising liquid over the shredded meat to make it moist, but not saucy.

Heat about 1 tablespoon (15 mL) of the olive oil in a large cast-iron skillet over high heat. Once the oil starts to shimmer, reduce the heat to medium. Working with one tortilla at a time, quickly submerge the shell into the braising liquid in the saucepan and then transfer it to the skillet. Fry for 1 to 2 minutes until the shell is crisp. Flip the shell and add ¼ to ½ cup (60 to 125 mL) of the shredded pork. Cook for 2 to 3 minutes, until the other side of the tortilla is crisp and the pork is warm. Sprinkle with cheese. Cook for 1 minute more. Transfer to a platter. Repeat with the remaining tortilla shells, using more olive oil in the skillet as needed.

Garnish with the cilantro, lime juice, white onion, jalapeño, and avocado. Serve with any remaining braising liquid on the side for dipping.

BRAISED BEEF NACHOS

SERVES 4

Something about the combination of crunchy chips, melty cheese, and spicy stuff is so widely appealing that I have yet to meet anyone who couldn't get on board with a platter of hot nachos. This version helps make use of leftover Braised Beef with Vinegar and Peppers (page 171) and pairs the rich beef with Monterey Jack cheese and pepperoncini. While those ingredients go into the oven with the chips to get hot and, in the cheese's case, melty, the thing that sets these nachos apart is all the great stuff you load on top after they come out of the oven—crunchy iceberg lettuce, herby cilantro, crispy radishes, and creamy avocado, all drizzled in Hot Vinegar (page 22) and lime juice.

2 cups (500 mL) or so leftover Braised Beef with Vinegar and Peppers (page 171), plus 1 cup (250 mL) braising liquid
4 to 5 cups (120 to 150 g) corn chips
7 ounces (200 g) shredded Monterey Jack or mozzarella cheese
1 cup (250 mL) pepperoncini, sliced

To serve
1 cup (250 mL) thinly sliced iceberg lettuce
½ bunch fresh cilantro, chopped
3 radishes, thinly sliced
1 avocado, pitted, peeled, and thinly sliced
2 tablespoons (30 mL) Hot Vinegar or pepperoncini brine
Juice of 1 lime
Hot sauce

Preheat the oven to 425°F (220°C).

Roughly chop the beef and peppers into bite-sized chunks. Place them in a small saucepan with the braising liquid. Bring the mixture to a boil over high heat. Reduce to a simmer, cooking for 4 to 5 minutes, until the liquid is reduced and the beef is tender.

Spread about half of the chips on a baking sheet, then spread about half of the beef, cheese, and pepperoncini evenly on top. Repeat with the remaining chips, beef, cheese, and pepperoncini.

Bake for 12 to 15 minutes, until the cheese is melted and bubbling. Let the nachos cool for 1 to 2 minutes. Sprinkle the lettuce, cilantro, radishes, and avocado on top. Drizzle with the hot vinegar and lime juice. Serve with hot sauce on the side.

Swap It: This recipe also works terrifically well with an equal amount of leftover Pepperoncini Braised Pork Shoulder (page 166) or even a roast chicken.

SERVES 4

CHILLED STEAK WITH EGGPLANT DIP, ARUGULA, AND PISTACHIOS

1 cup (250 mL) Charred Eggplant Dip with Hot Honey and Toasted Sesame (page 45)
4 ounces (115 g) or so Steak Night Steak (page 203), chilled and thinly sliced
2 tablespoons (30 mL) Honey Harissa (page 25), more for drizzling
2 cups (500 mL) baby arugula
¼ cup (60 mL) pistachios, toasted
Extra-virgin olive oil, for drizzling

Combining a number of different leftovers and pairing them with a smart condiment is a great strategy for making a meal in a hurry. Here, leftover steak gets a makeover when it's plunked into creamy eggplant dip, drizzled with Honey Harissa (page 25), and then given a bit of a lift with peppery arugula and crunchy pistachios.

The ingredients list here is short, but if you try this recipe, you'll find that everything in the dish works in harmony. All the textures you might wish for in a satisfying meal are well represented. Since there is nothing to cook (unless you decide to make parts of it fresh), you can make this in about five minutes. This dish also offers flexibility—you can make it more meaty or more salad-y depending on what you have on hand and your personal preferences. I love this dish served as a quick summer dinner with a few warm Turkish or pita breads and a chilled glass of fruity red wine.

Place a large platter in the freezer to chill.

Use a large spoon to dollop the eggplant dip on the chilled platter and then smooth it around the plate into a rough oval shape. Pile the steak on top. Spoon the honey harissa overtop. Pile the arugula on the steak. Sprinkle the pistachios over everything. Drizzle all over with olive oil, and add a little more honey harissa, if desired. Serve shortly after plating. If you would like to wait, hold off on dressing the greens until right before you are ready to eat. You may be serving leftovers, but if you heap a lovely big pile of greens on top, no one has to know except us.

Swap It: Please, please get on board with bitter greens (page 100) and try swapping out the arugula for radicchio. Alternatively, spinach, romaine, and even baby kale are all great options.

McCall's

HERBY SLICED STEAK WITH FETA, BABY GEM, AND RADISHES

SERVES 4

Next to pepperoni and mozzarella, I think steak and feta might just be my favourite meat 'n' cheese combo. Something about the marriage of juicy steak and creamy, salty feta hits all my tastebuds and makes for a really compelling start to a delicious dish. Here I layer on the fresh flavours—baby gem lettuce, peppery radishes, and crisp onion—and add a healthy pour of Green Crunch Sauce (page 30) to bring everything together. A little sumac adds a bit of acidity to this dish, but if you don't have it, don't worry, just add an extra drizzle of Everyday Vinegar (page 21) or, if you're feeling spicy, Hot Vinegar (page 22).

½ small yellow onion, thinly sliced
4 ounces (115 g) or so Steak Night Steak (page 203), chilled and thinly sliced
4 ounces (115 g) feta, crumbled
3 heads baby gem lettuce, leaves separated
6 radishes, quartered
½ cup (125 mL) Green Crunch Sauce (page 30)
Pinch of ground sumac
Fresh cracked black pepper

Place the onion in a small bowl of ice water and let soak for at least 5 minutes to take out the sting.

Place the steak, feta, lettuce, radishes, onion, green crunch sauce, sumac, and pepper to taste in a large metal bowl. Toss until everything is well coated and jumbled together nicely. Serve immediately.

Swap It: Sumac is a tart red spice that I will often reach for instead of fresh citrus to add acidity and brightness to a dish. If you don't have it on hand, just add an extra splash of white vinegar or a squeeze of lemon or lime.

DON'T STRESS OVER DESSERT

SWEET THINGS THAT COME TOGETHER EASILY are essential not just for entertaining but for a happy life. This chapter includes a range of desserts perfect for the novice baker that aren't demanding in terms of time or effort: some don't even involve turning on the oven. You won't need any fancy equipment here, although a blender and a stand mixer do help, but my personal dessert style is what I like to call grandma-gourmet, and that limits the fuss required and focuses on flavour instead.

In this chapter you'll find dessert recipes for every mood, whether you're looking for the perfect (yes I said it) Double Raisin Oatmeal Cookies (page 241), rich Sesame Chocolate Pots de Crème with Honey Whip and Sesame Snaps (page 251) that come together in about five minutes of cook time, or a simple Any Fruit Cake (page 265) recipe that's very good as written but also accommodates the introduction of whatever fruit is in season, including and especially tinned pineapple.

DOUBLE RAISIN OATMEAL COOKIES

MAKES ABOUT 12 MEDIUM COOKIES

This is such a fun recipe because you get to sink your teeth into two textures of raisins—chewy dried raisins, which are so satisfying, and then softer, plump soaked raisins, whose flavour is a wonderful complement to the hearty, oaty, and coconutty cookie base. Rich molasses adds depth here, and there is just enough cinnamon to add warmth and spice. Refrigerating the dough helps the flavours commingle and is one of those touches that doesn't require anything but time, yet elevates this recipe to new heights.

2 cups (250 mL) golden raisins, divided
1 cup (250 mL/225 g) unsalted butter
1 cup (250 mL) light brown sugar
1 tablespoon (15 mL) fancy molasses
2 eggs
1 tablespoon (15 mL) pure vanilla extract
1½ cups (375 mL) all-purpose flour
1 teaspoon (5 mL) baking soda
2 teaspoons (10 mL) cinnamon
1 teaspoon (5 mL) salt
2 cups (500 mL) rolled oats
1 cup (250 mL) unsweetened shredded coconut

Place 1 cup (250 mL) of the golden raisins in a small heatproof bowl. Cover with boiling water and set aside.

In the bowl of a stand mixer fitted with the paddle attachment, cream together the butter and brown sugar for 2 to 3 minutes, until light and fluffy. Add the molasses. Beat until just combined. With the mixer running on medium speed, add the eggs, one at a time, until they are fully incorporated. Add the vanilla and beat briefly to combine.

In a medium bowl, use a fine-mesh sieve to sift together the flour, baking soda, and cinnamon. Sprinkle the salt into the dry mixture. Stir to combine.

Gently add about half the dry ingredients to the wet ingredients. Mix on low speed until just combined. Add the remaining dry ingredients. Mix until just combined. Drain the water from the bowl of raisins. Add the soaked raisins, unsoaked raisins, oats, and coconut to the bowl of the stand mixer. Mix until a dough forms. Wrap the dough tightly in plastic wrap. Refrigerate for at least 2 hours or overnight.

Preheat the oven to 375°F (190°C). Line 2 baking sheets with parchment paper.

With your hands, form the cookie dough into 2-inch (5 cm) balls. Arrange the dough balls on the prepared baking sheets, evenly spaced. Press each ball to flatten until each cookie is about ¾ inch (2 cm) thick. Bake for 11 to 12 minutes, or until golden brown. Transfer the cookies to a wire rack to cool completely.

Store the cookies in an airtight container at room temperature for up to 1 week.

Tip: If you don't have a fine-mesh sieve, you can place all the dry ingredients in a large bowl and use your hands to gently massage and sift them together. This makes the flour less dense, and breaks up any baking soda lumps that may be lurking in your dry ingredients.

MAKES ONE 10-INCH BUNDT CAKE

MARASCHINO CHERRY POUND CAKE

Pound Cake

- 3¾ cups (925 mL) + 1 tablespoon (15 mL) all-purpose flour
- 1 tablespoon (15 mL) baking powder
- 1 teaspoon (5 mL) baking soda
- 1 teaspoon (5 mL) kosher salt
- 1½ cups (375 mL/340 g) unsalted butter, room temperature
- 2 cups (500 mL) granulated sugar
- Zest of 1 lemon
- 4 eggs, room temperature
- 1 tablespoon (15 mL) pure vanilla extract
- 1 cup + 2 tablespoons (280 mL) whole (3.25%) milk
- Juice of 1 lemon
- 2 tablespoons (30 mL) white vinegar
- 2 jars (375 mL each) maraschino cherries, drained, plus 1 tablespoon (15 mL) syrup reserved for glaze

Glaze

- 1 tablespoon (15 mL) reserved maraschino cherry syrup (see above)
- 2 cups (500 mL) icing sugar
- 3 tablespoons (45 mL) whole (3.25%) milk or heavy (35%) cream
- A few drops of red food colouring (optional)

This is not an overly sweet cake, and the addition of bright, juicy maraschino cherries creates a wonderful contrast in texture and flavour. It's essentially a giant pound cake, and therefore not overwhelming to make, but because it's baked in a bundt pan and then glazed, it feels pretty glamorous.

Make the Pound Cake: Preheat the oven to 350°F (180°C). Grease and flour a 10-inch (3 L) bundt pan (see Tip).

In a medium bowl, sift together 3¾ cups (925 mL) of the flour, the baking powder, and the baking soda. Add the salt. Use a whisk to give the dry ingredients a final mix.

In the bowl of a stand mixer fitted with the paddle attachment, cream together the butter, sugar, and lemon zest for 2 to 3 minutes on high speed, until light and fluffy. With the mixer running on low, add the eggs, one at a time, until fully incorporated. Add in the vanilla and mix again briefly.

Add about half of the flour mixture to the wet ingredients. Mix until just combined. In a small bowl, whisk together the milk, lemon juice, and vinegar. Add about half of the milk mixture to the stand mixer bowl. Mix briefly to combine. Repeat these two steps, adding the dry ingredients first, followed by the wet ingredients, being careful not to overmix or the cake will be tough.

Spoon 1 tablespoon (15 mL) reserved cherry syrup into a medium bowl and set aside. Drain any remaining syrup from the cherries using a fine-mesh sieve. Sprinkle the remaining 1 tablespoon (15 mL) flour overtop of the cherries. Toss to coat them in flour to prevent them from sinking to the bottom of the cake. Gently stir the cherries into the cake batter.

Use a rubber spatula to scrape the batter into the prepared bundt pan. Bake for 60 to 70 minutes, or until golden brown and a cake tester inserted into the middle comes out clean. Let cool in the pan for 10 minutes. Carefully invert the cake onto a wire rack. Let cool to room temperature.

Make the Glaze: In the medium bowl containing the cherry syrup, add the icing sugar, milk, and food colouring (if using). Whisk until smooth. Pour the glaze over the cooled cake. Serve.

Store the cake in an airtight container in the fridge for up to 5 days.

Tip: Bundt pans need a little extra TLC in the prep phase so that the cake comes out smoothly. I like to use a pastry brush and lots of soft butter to grease the pan, and then I put about ¼ cup (60 mL) flour in the cake pan and, turning it on its side over a bowl, rotate it all around so that the flour sticks to the butter and coats the inside of the bundt pan.

Tip: If you don't have frozen raspberries, feel free to use store-bought jam or chocolate sauce instead of making the jam.

You can freeze this dessert, but I recommend keeping the components separate and assembling just before serving. Warm the thawed profiteroles for about 3 minutes in a 350°F (180°C) oven before stuffing them with filling.

RASPBERRY JAM AND VANILLA ICE CREAM PROFITEROLES

MAKES 6 TO 7 PROFITEROLES

This dessert—rich, golden pastries stuffed with creamy vanilla ice cream and a tart raspberry jam—looks and sounds fancy, but once you make it, you'll see how quickly it comes together and how popular it is with everyone. Make these for your next backyard party, or on a hot summer day, or basically for any event where something resembling a giant ice cream sandwich will go over well.

Raspberry Jam (see Tip)

- 1 cup (250 mL) frozen raspberries
- 1 tablespoon (15 mL) chia seeds
- 1 tablespoon (15 mL) pure maple syrup

Profiterole Pastry

- 1 cup (250 mL) water
- ½ cup (125 mL) butter
- Pinch of salt
- 2 tablespoons (30 mL) sugar
- 1 cup (250 mL) all-purpose flour
- 4 to 5 eggs

To serve

- 3 cups (750 mL) vanilla ice cream
- Icing sugar, for dusting

Make the Raspberry Jam: In a small bowl, stir together the raspberries, chia seeds, and maple syrup. Place in the fridge to set while you make the puffs.

Make the Profiteroles: Preheat the oven to 400°F (200°C). Line a medium baking sheet with parchment paper.

In a medium saucepan over high heat, stir together the water, butter, salt, and sugar, until the butter melts and the sugar dissolves. Add the flour and, using a wooden spoon, stir briskly to keep the flour from sticking to the bottom as it combines with the water to form a dough. Reduce the heat to medium-high. Continue stirring until the dough becomes quite stiff, 2 to 3 minutes. Remove the saucepan from the heat.

Using the wooden spoon, beat in 4 of the eggs, one at a time, until they are fully absorbed. The dough should be shiny, thick, and able to hold its shape when it's spooned onto the baking sheet. If the dough is too stiff, you may need to add one additional egg, or even just the yolk if they are on the larger side.

Dip a pastry brush in water. Brush it over the prepared baking sheet to moisten the parchment paper. This will help the pastry rise. Spoon the dough out into 6 or 7 mounds, spacing them out evenly on the tray so they have room to expand. Bake for 20 to 25 minutes, until they are nicely puffed and golden brown. Use a toothpick or metal skewer to poke a small hole in the side of each pastry ball so that the steam can escape, and transfer to a wire rack to cool.

Assemble the Profiteroles: Use a serrated knife to slice each puff like you would a sandwich bun, leaving enough puff to make a sort of hinge on one side. Put a good-size scoop of ice cream in each profiterole. Spoon some raspberry jam on top. Close the puffs so the top half sits on the ice cream. Sift a little powdered sugar on top. Serve immediately.

I DREAM OF TAHINI: THE DESSERT INGREDIENT I CAN'T LIVE WITHOUT

Tahini is a paste made of sesame seeds, and it has a wonderful rich, nutty flavour with just a hint of pleasant bitterness. It's relatively inexpensive compared to other nut and seed butters, and can be used interchangeably in most recipes. As with all your ingredients, there is a real spectrum in terms of price and quality when it comes to tahini, but it's worth it to find the best quality you can—cheaper versions can taste too bitter or even rancid. I opt for a version made by Parallel Brothers in Toronto: they ensure that the sesame seeds used to make it are ground fresh, the texture is creamy, and the flavour is balanced. Tahini adds wonderful depth and what I like to call a gentle bitterness that balances sweet flavours. If you're not yet folding it into your sweet cravings, here are some recipes to get you started.

MAKES ONE 8-INCH (2 L) SQUARE CAKE

WARM DATE CAKE WITH TAHINI DULCE DE LECHE

Dulce de Leche (see Tip)

1 can (300 mL/400 g) sweetened condensed milk
2 tablespoons (30 mL) tahini
Pinch of salt (optional)

Date Cake

¾ cup (175 mL) chopped pitted Medjool dates
¾ cup (175 mL) coffee or water (see Tip)
1 teaspoon (5 mL) baking soda
6 tablespoons (90 mL) unsalted butter
2 tablespoons (30 mL) tahini
¾ cup (175 mL) sugar
1 teaspoon (5 mL) salt
2 eggs
1½ cups (375 mL) all-purpose flour

To serve

Sesame seeds, toasted
Vanilla ice cream or whipped cream (optional)

This is a riff on an old classic: sticky toffee pudding. Like sticky toffee pudding, it's a warm, date-studded cake covered in a luscious sauce. It differs, however, in that this cake uses tahini to give it a slightly bolder flavour, and I use a no-fuss dulce de leche sauce that also incorporates a little tahini to temper the sweetness. If you've never tried dates and tahini before, they really are a natural pairing—tahini and date syrup slathered on toast is an Egyptian-style breakfast my daughters love—and you'll find that this dessert, especially when topped with a smattering of crunchy sesame seeds, showcases both ingredients in a way that feels at once familiar and exciting.

Start the Dulce de Leche: Take the label off the can of condensed milk. Fill a medium saucepan with water. Place the closed can in the water, making sure the water covers the can completely, and by at least 1 inch (2.5 cm).

Bring the water to a boil over high heat. Reduce the heat to a simmer. Let the can simmer, uncovered, for about 2 hours, occasionally topping up the water so the can remains submerged. Remove the can from the water and set aside to cool while you bake the cake. Do not open the can while it's hot to the touch or the contents will squirt everywhere.

Make the Date Cake: Preheat the oven to 350°F (180°C). Lightly grease an 8-inch (2 L) square pan.

In a medium saucepan, bring the dates and coffee to a boil over high heat. Turn off the heat. Add the baking soda. The mixture will darken and foam up, but that's normal. Just give it a whisk and set it aside to cool.

In the bowl of a stand mixer fitted with the paddle attachment, cream together the butter, tahini, and sugar for 2 to 3 minutes, until light and fluffy. Add the salt. With the mixer running on medium speed, add the eggs one at a time, until fully incorporated. Add the date mixture to the egg mixture and mix briefly. Add the flour and mix again until just combined. Transfer the batter to the prepared pan. Bake for 18 to 20 minutes, until the cake is golden brown and a cake tester comes out clean.

Use a skewer to poke holes all over the cake. Open the can of condensed milk and transfer it to a small bowl. Whisk in the tahini and a pinch of salt (if using). Pour the dulce de leche all over the cake and allow it to seep in for 2 to 3 minutes. Serve warm with sesame seeds sprinkled on top, and vanilla ice cream or whipped cream if you choose.

Store leftovers in an airtight container in the fridge for up to 5 days.

Tip: A lot of sticky toffee pudding recipes call for water, but I typically have a cold cup of coffee floating around my fridge, and I use it here to bring more flavour and a touch of richness. Coffee works well in lieu of water in darker cakes like chocolate, rum, or even poppy seed.

SESAME CHOCOLATE POTS DE CRÈME WITH HONEY WHIP AND SESAME SNAPS

MAKES 8 POTS DE CRÈME

Slipping a little of my favourite sesame seed paste into this classic velvety chocolate dessert adds both nuance and an even richer texture. It also makes it taste like the filling of a 3 Musketeers bar. The combination of softly whipped cream and crunchy shards of Sesame Snap makes this dessert both elegant and nostalgic, so it's always a crowd-pleaser. Plate this dish individually in vintage teacups, coupe glasses, or ramekins—or create a single large-format pot de crème by setting it in a medium shallow bowl or platter.

- 2½ cups (625 mL) + ¾ cup (175 mL) heavy (35%) cream, divided
- 6 egg yolks (see Tip)
- 2 tablespoons (30 mL) sugar
- Pinch of salt
- 9 ounces (255 g) milk chocolate
- 2 tablespoons (30 mL) tahini
- 1 tablespoon (15 mL) pure liquid honey
- 2 packets (30 g each) Sesame Snaps

In a medium saucepan over medium heat, combine 2½ cups (625 mL) of the cream, the egg yolks, the sugar, and the salt. Whisk to combine. Using a spatula, stir briskly while the yolks thicken. Continue stirring until the mixture coats the back of a spoon. Remove from the heat.

Place the chocolate and tahini in a high-speed blender. Pour the cream mixture overtop. Turn the blender on low speed and gradually increase the speed to high. Let the blender run on high for about 2 minutes, until everything is fully combined and smooth. Divide the mixture evenly among 8 individual ramekins or cups. Place them in the refrigerator to set for at least 4 hours or overnight.

In a large metal bowl, vigorously whisk the remaining ¾ cup (175 mL) of cream and the honey until soft peaks form. Whip for 1 more minute.

Place the Sesame Snap packets on a hard surface. Give each one a whack or two with a rolling pin. Use scissors to cut open the packets and place the contents in a small bowl. Garnish each pot de crème with a dollop of whipped cream and a sprinkle of crushed Sesame Snaps.

Tip: Egg whites freeze terrifically well in a small airtight container. Simply thaw them and use as directed to make Pistachio Cookies (page 255) or as an egg wash for Cod Cakes with Dilly Mayo (page 209).

TAHINI BASQUE CHEESECAKE

MAKES ONE 12-INCH (30 CM) CHEESECAKE

- 1½ pounds (675 g) plain cream cheese, room temperature
- ½ cup (125 mL) tahini
- 1½ cups (375 mL) sugar
- Pinch of salt
- 1½ cups (375 mL) heavy (35%) cream
- 6 eggs, beaten
- 1 tablespoon (15 mL) all-purpose flour
- 1 tablespoon (15 mL) cornstarch

At one of my first bakery jobs, I used to dread making cheesecakes. We made this dessert New York style and, after packing the crust and then pouring the liquidy cake filling into a springform pan, we baked the cakes in a water bath. Sometimes the pans leaked, other times the cakes cracked, and it was all very stressful and anxiety-inducing, which really undermined the pleasure of biting into a silky, delicious cheesecake! This version, however, skips the crust, gets baked right in a cast-iron pan without a water bath, and is incredibly forgiving. Even if you have never baked before, trust me, you can make this and it will be perfect!

Preheat the oven to 400°F (200°C). Line a 12-inch (30 cm) cast-iron skillet with high sides with parchment paper that has been cut to fit the width of the pan with a few inches of overhang for easy removal.

In a stand mixer fitted with a paddle attachment, beat the cream cheese and tahini for 4 to 5 minutes, until smooth. Add the sugar and salt. Beat for 2 to 3 minutes, until fully mixed. Add the cream. Beat for 1 minute. Add the eggs, flour, and cornstarch. Mix until just combined.

Transfer the cheesecake batter to the prepared cast-iron skillet. Bake on the oven's middle rack for 40 minutes. Adjust the heat to broil. Cook for 1 minute more, until the top is golden brown. Let cool to room temperature. Refrigerate for 4 hours.

Use the parchment paper to lift the cheesecake out of the pan and onto a cutting board. Cut slices using a hot wet knife.

Store leftovers in an airtight container in the fridge for up to 1 week.

Castle Theatre
ESKÝ KRUMLOV

PISTACHIO COOKIES

MAKES 8 COOKIES

These cookies are crispy, chewy, and quite addictive, and have the benefit of being a great way to use up egg whites you may have left over from a recipe that uses only yolks. I've scaled this recipe to use just one egg white, but you can easily double, triple, or, if you've just made Sesame Chocolate Pots de Crème with Honey Whip and Sesame Snaps (page 251), sextuple (!) this recipe.

⅔ cup (150 mL) pistachios
⅓ cup (75 mL) sugar
Pinch of salt
1 egg white

Preheat the oven to 350°F (180°C). Line a medium baking sheet with parchment paper.

Place the pistachios, sugar, and salt in a high-speed blender or food processor. Pulse until the nuts are finely ground. Scrape the contents of the blender into a medium bowl. Add the egg white. Use a spatula to mix until fully combined.

Using a metal spoon, drop about eight 2-tablespoon (30 mL) dollops of batter onto the prepared baking sheet. Bake for 12 to 14 minutes, until golden brown and crispy. Transfer the cookies to a wire rack to cool.

Store in an airtight container in a cool, dry place for up to 4 days. They will lose some of their crispiness, but are still a very good cookie.

Tip: I freeze my egg whites until I am ready to use them. Simply thaw in the fridge and use as you would normally.

MAPLE BUTTERMILK PANNA COTTA WITH CINNAMON TOAST CRUMBLES AND BLUEBERRIES

SERVES 8

Buttermilk has a terrific acidity and is great for adding creaminess to chilled soups (page 123) or drizzling on hearty stews. When it comes to desserts, it's often used to give extra lift to cakes and muffins, but its refreshing quality can be lost. In this dessert, however, where it is incorporated into a classic panna cotta and paired with cinnamon toast crumbles and a little drizzle of maple syrup, we really let the buttermilk *be the buttermilk*, and it shines—in all of its tart, creamy glory.

Panna Cotta

4 sheets (2 g each) gelatin (see Tip)
1 cup (250 mL) plain full-fat Greek yogurt or labneh
1 cup (250 mL) buttermilk
2 cups (500 mL) heavy (35%) cream
1 cup (250 mL) pure maple syrup, more for drizzling

Cinnamon Toast Crumbles

2 slices white sandwich bread
2 tablespoons (30 mL) unsalted butter
Pinch of salt
2 tablespoons (30 mL) light brown sugar
1 teaspoon cinnamon

To serve

1 cup (250 mL) blueberries
Pure maple syrup, for drizzling

Make the Panna Cotta: Place the gelatin sheets in a medium bowl of cold water. If you use warm water, the gelatin will melt, and all we're looking to do here is bloom it, meaning let it absorb the cold water. Set aside while you make the panna cotta.

In a small bowl, whisk together the yogurt and buttermilk.

In a small saucepan over high heat, warm the cream until it just starts to boil. Turn off the heat. Use your hands to remove the gelatin from the water and squeeze it to remove any excess. Whisk the gelatin into the hot cream.

Pour about a third of the hot cream into the buttermilk mixture. Whisk to combine. Pour about a third of that mixture back into the hot cream and whisk to combine. Finally, pour all the cream mixture into the buttermilk mixture and give a final whisk.

Divide the panna cotta evenly among 8 small bowls, ramekins, or teacups. Place them in the fridge to set for at least 2 hours.

Make the Cinnamon Toast Crumbles: Toast the bread in a toaster. Roughly chop the toast into large bread crumbs. Do not try to make the crumbs into perfect squares; they look and taste better when they are a bit shaggy and clearly homemade.

In a large skillet over medium-high heat, melt the butter. Add the salt and brown sugar. Add the chopped toast and let it cook for 3 to 4 minutes, until it absorbs all of the good flavours and turns golden brown all over. Sprinkle with the cinnamon. Stir to coat evenly. Turn off the heat and let cool.

To serve: Top each dish of panna cotta with a handful of blueberries, a spoonful of cinnamon toast crumbles, and a drizzle of maple syrup. Serve immediately.

SERVES 6 TO 8

JAMMY BLUEBERRIES WITH LEMON DUMPLINGS

Blueberry Filling

5 cups (1.25 L) fresh or frozen blueberries, divided (see Swap It)

¼ cup (60 mL) sugar

Pinch of cinnamon

1 tablespoon (15 mL) water

Pinch of salt

Juice of 1 lemon

Dumplings

2 cups (500 mL) all-purpose flour

2 teaspoons (10 mL) baking powder

1 teaspoon (5 mL) baking soda

1 tablespoon (15 mL) sugar

Pinch of salt

Zest of 1 lemon

1 cup (250 mL) whole (3.25%) milk

3 tablespoons (45 mL) melted butter

To serve

Vanilla ice cream

Pure maple syrup, for drizzling

Growing up in Nova Scotia and the United Kingdom, I noticed that some of the most delicious foods have the strangest names, ones that aren't particularly appetite-inducing: toad in the hole, bubble and squeak, scrapple, fool, flummery—even flapjacks (something about the word "flap" is a real turnoff for me). While many of these recipes make their way into modern cookbooks with their names intact, not all of them sound tempting to the modern reader.

This recipe would be called blueberry grunt by anyone on the East Coast, but I wouldn't want you to be deterred from making this simple but stunning combo of jammy blueberries and soft lemony dumplings simply because "grunt" fails to be a compelling dessert word. Make this in the summer when blueberries are in season for a big al fresco dinner, or use frozen blueberries in the winter for a really cozy family meal that deserves a warm dumpling finish.

Make the Blueberry Filling: In a large Dutch oven over high heat, place about half of the blueberries, the sugar, cinnamon, water, salt, and lemon juice. Cook for 3 to 5 minutes, stirring occasionally, until the berries burst. Add the remaining blueberries. Reduce the heat to a simmer while you make the dumplings.

Make the Dumplings: In a medium bowl, whisk together the flour, baking powder, baking soda, sugar, salt, and lemon zest. In a separate medium bowl, whisk together the milk and melted butter. Pour the wet ingredients into the dry ingredients. Use a rubber spatula to stir until just combined. Use a large tablespoon to drop the dough into the saucepan of blueberries. You'll get about 6 large spoonfuls: be sure to space them out when adding to the blueberries so they have room to expand. Once all the dough has been added, cover and let steam over low heat for 20 minutes, resisting the urge to remove the lid and peek, until the dumplings are puffed and a paring knife inserted into the centre of the dumplings comes out hot to the touch. Serve immediately with vanilla ice cream and a drizzle of maple syrup.

Leftovers will inevitably turn quite blue but can be stored in an airtight container in the fridge for up to 5 days.

Tip: While this is technically a dessert, it also makes a very good breakfast, especially when whipped up during peak blueberry season over a campfire.

Swap It: Although a grunt is typically blueberry-based, there's no rule to say you can't use an equal amount of peaches, cherries, apples, or any other fruit that would suit a cobbler or crisp-type dessert.

PHYLLO CRINKLE CAKE

MAKES ONE 13 X 9-INCH (3.5 L) CAKE

- 1½ to 2 boxes (1½ to 2 pounds/675 to 900 g) phyllo pastry
- 1 cup (250 mL) melted unsalted butter
- Pinch of salt, more for sprinkling
- 1 can (300 mL/400 g) sweetened condensed milk
- 1 cup (250 mL) heavy (35%) cream
- ¼ cup (60 mL) hot honey
- ¼ cup (60 mL) chopped pistachios (see Swap It)

I tend to use phyllo more often in savoury dishes, like Phyllo Wrapped Feta with Hot Honey (page 181) or some sort of free-form spanakopita. I tend to find, though, that any recipe I make leaves me with most of a box of phyllo in my fridge. While I always have good intentions to use it, it inevitably goes stiff and I have to chuck it in the trash. For me, a person who doesn't like to waste anything, that is a problem, and for that problem, this recipe is the solution. It is flexible enough to absorb anywhere from 1½ to 2 boxes of phyllo, and it yields a buttery, honeyed, flaky, and nutty dessert that looks complicated but is about as challenging to make as a folded paper fan.

Preheat the oven to 375°F (190°C). Lightly grease a 13 x 9-inch (3.5 L) baking dish.

To the left of your work area, place the phyllo pastry in a stack, loosely covered with a clean and damp—but not wet—kitchen towel. Place the baking dish to the right of your work area. Add a pinch of salt to the melted butter. Place it at the top of your work area.

Take one sheet of phyllo and place it in front of you lengthwise. Use a pastry brush to brush lightly with the melted butter. Fold the sheet up from bottom to top, accordion style, as if you are making a paper fan with the folds about 2 inches (5 cm) wide. Place the accordion in the prepared baking dish lengthwise with the folds up—it should just fit. Repeat the process of brushing and folding with the remaining sheets of phyllo, one at a time, and fill the dish. It should be quite a snug fit, and the nice thing about this recipe is that a little more or less phyllo won't be noticeable; the whole thing should look a bit wild and craggy. Pour any remaining butter overtop.

Bake for 20 minutes, until the phyllo is golden brown. Remove the baking dish from the oven and pour the condensed milk, cream, and hot honey evenly overtop. Return to the oven and bake for another 10 to 15 minutes, until the liquid is bubbling and caramelized. Sprinkle with pistachios and additional salt, if desired. Serve warm.

Store leftovers in an airtight container in the fridge for up to 5 days.

Swap It: If you don't have or don't want to use pistachios for this recipe, toasted sesame seeds are also wonderful!

MAKES ONE 8-INCH (2 L) SQUARE CAKE

- 1½ cups (375 mL) all-purpose flour
- 1 cup (250 mL) sugar
- 3 tablespoons (45 mL) cocoa powder
- 1 tablespoon (15 mL) black cocoa powder (see Tip)
- 1 teaspoon (5 mL) baking soda
- 1 teaspoon (5 mL) salt
- 5 tablespoons (75 mL) melted butter or olive oil
- 1 tablespoon (15 mL) white vinegar
- 1 teaspoon (5 mL) pure vanilla extract
- 1 cup (250 mL) cold coffee or water
- Whipped cream or vanilla ice cream, to serve
- Icing sugar, for dusting

WACKY CAKE

Wacky cake, a light, chocolatey cake that tastes a bit like it came from a box mix—in a good way—has somewhat murky origins. Most people think it was created during the Great Depression or the Second World War, when eggs were hard to come by and butter was expensive. It became popular again in the 1980s and '90s as an option for people who didn't particularly like spending time in the kitchen, since it takes only moments to mix together. Economy and efficiency are two things I love in a homemade dessert, so I'm bringing Wacky Cake back into the spotlight where it belongs. The original recipe and many other Wacky Cake recipes call for canola or vegetable oil, and you can certainly stick with that, but I opt for a little luxury in the form of melted butter instead.

Preheat the oven to 350°F (180°C). Lightly grease an 8-inch (2 L) square baking pan.

In a medium bowl, whisk together the flour, sugar, cocoa powder, black cocoa powder, baking soda, and salt.

In a small bowl, whisk together the melted butter, white vinegar, vanilla, and coffee. Pour the wet ingredients into the dry ingredients and use a rubber spatula to mix until they are just combined. Use the same spatula to transfer the batter to the prepared pan. Smooth the top. Bake for 25 to 30 minutes or until a cake tester inserted in the middle comes out clean. Top with whipped cream or vanilla ice cream and a dusting of icing sugar.

Store leftovers in an airtight container in the fridge for up to 5 days.

Tip: Black cocoa powder results in a really rich, dark cake. If you don't have it, simply use an additional 1 tablespoon (15 mL) of regular cocoa powder. The cake will taste just as good.

ANY FRUIT CAKE

MAKES ONE 8-INCH (2 L) SQUARE CAKE

- 1½ cups (375 mL) all-purpose flour
- 1 cup (250 mL) sugar
- 2 teaspoons (10 mL) baking powder
- 1 teaspoon (5 mL) baking soda
- 1 teaspoon (5 mL) salt
- 1 cup (250 mL) full-fat sour cream or plain yogurt
- Zest and juice of 1 lemon
- 2 teaspoons (10 mL) pure vanilla extract
- 3 eggs
- ½ cup (125 mL) melted butter, cooled, or olive oil

Cake and fruit are very good together, and I love this recipe because it lends itself to all kinds of fruits. Summer fruits like peaches and plums work well; so do fall fruits like apples and pears, and even winter fruits like citrus and frozen blueberries. What follows is the recipe for a superb vanilla-flavoured, lightly lemoned cake that is wonderful as is but also allows for so many variations. I've made some suggestions for variations on the following page, and my hope is that once you have made a cake or two, you will gain the confidence to create combinations of your own. As long as you keep the volume of liquid, flour, sugar, fat, and fruit the same, you will likely be successful. But if you go really off-script and start throwing in cantaloupe or dragon fruit, I cannot guarantee results.

Preheat the oven to 350°F (180°C). Lightly grease an 8-inch (2 L) square baking dish.

In a medium bowl, whisk together the flour, sugar, baking powder, baking soda, and salt.

In a small bowl, whisk together the sour cream, lemon zest and juice, vanilla, eggs, and melted butter. Pour the wet ingredients into the dry ingredients and use a rubber spatula to stir until just combined. Use the spatula to transfer the batter to the prepared baking dish. Smooth the top. Bake for 1 hour or until a cake tester comes out clean. Let cool and serve.

Tip: This cake goes very well with whipped cream and some fresh raspberries that have sat in a cool place with a splash of rosé and a large pinch of sugar until they have given up their juice. Alternatively, a thin layer of jam or marmalade spread on top of the cake will add some luxury, or you can whisk together about 1 cup (250 mL) of icing sugar and the juice of 1 lemon to make a simple, effective glaze.

SWAP IT

BLUEBERRY CAKE

Toss 1½ cups (375 mL) frozen blueberries in 1 tablespoon (15 mL) all-purpose flour. Fold the blueberries into the batter just before transferring it to the prepared baking dish. Bake as directed.

PINEAPPLE UPSIDE DOWN CAKE

Instead of greasing the 8-inch (2 L) square baking dish, pour about ¼ cup (60 mL) melted butter into the bottom and then sprinkle ½ cup (125 mL) light brown sugar on top. Arrange 4 to 5 slices of fresh or tinned pineapple in a single layer on the bottom of the dish and dot it with maraschino cherries. Make the cake as directed, substituting 2 tablespoons (30 mL) pineapple juice for the lemon juice and zest. Bake as directed. Let cool in the pan for 10 minutes before inverting onto a cooling rack.

PLUM AND WALNUT CAKE

When preparing the dry ingredients, substitute ½ cup (125 mL) finely ground walnuts for ½ cup of the all-purpose flour. When preparing the wet ingredients, substitute 2 teaspoons (10 mL) bourbon or rum for the vanilla. Make the batter and transfer it to the prepared dish. Tear about 4 plums into bite-sized chunks and sprinkle them onto the surface of the batter, followed by ¼ cup (60 mL) light brown sugar that you have mixed with 1 teaspoon (5 mL) cinnamon and a pinch of salt. Bake as directed.

ORANGE AND SEMOLINA CAKE

Grease the baking dish as normal, then line the baking dish with about 9 thin slices of orange before making the batter. When preparing the dry ingredients, use 1 cup (250 mL) semolina and ½ cup (125 mL) ground almonds instead of the all-purpose flour. With the wet ingredients, use the zest and juice of ½ an orange instead of lemon, and use 2 teaspoons (10 mL) limoncello, lemon extract, or lemon-flavoured vodka instead of vanilla. Bake as directed. Let cool in the pan for 10 minutes before inverting onto a cooling rack.

THE

ACKNOWLEDGMENTS

Thanks to everyone who made this book possible. Cookbooks take a tremendously long time, and this one has turned into a five-year project—a bit ironic, given my emphasis on speedy recipes!

I owe a huge debt of gratitude to my team—Chris, Alyssa, Lindsay, and Andrea. We really make beautiful books together and it's been an honour working with you. The amount I have learned from each of you is unquantifiable.

To the team at Penguin: Marion Garner, Alanna McMullen, and Brittany Larkin thanks for putting it all together. To Laura Dosky and Lorissa Sengara especially: thanks for your patience and careful polish of this manuscript.

Thank you to all my cooking class students! You were often unknowing guinea pigs for these recipes and offered direct and honest feedback, as well as suggestions. I really wrote this book with you all in mind. Finally! You have the basil oil recipe!

To all my coworkers, past and present, and especially the team at GE, this book wouldn't exist without you. Or maybe it would, but the recipes wouldn't be nearly as delicious. I hope these dishes flood you with not just flavour but memories of big laughs, goofy dance parties (hey Mario!), and eating delicious things mid-service while standing over trashcans.

To my parents: thanks for normalizing delicious dinners as the standard and for showing me that cooking is both a pleasure and a gift you can share.

Thank you finally to my husband and daughters, who offer unwavering support and thoughtful critiques, and are always willing to eat leftovers.

INDEX